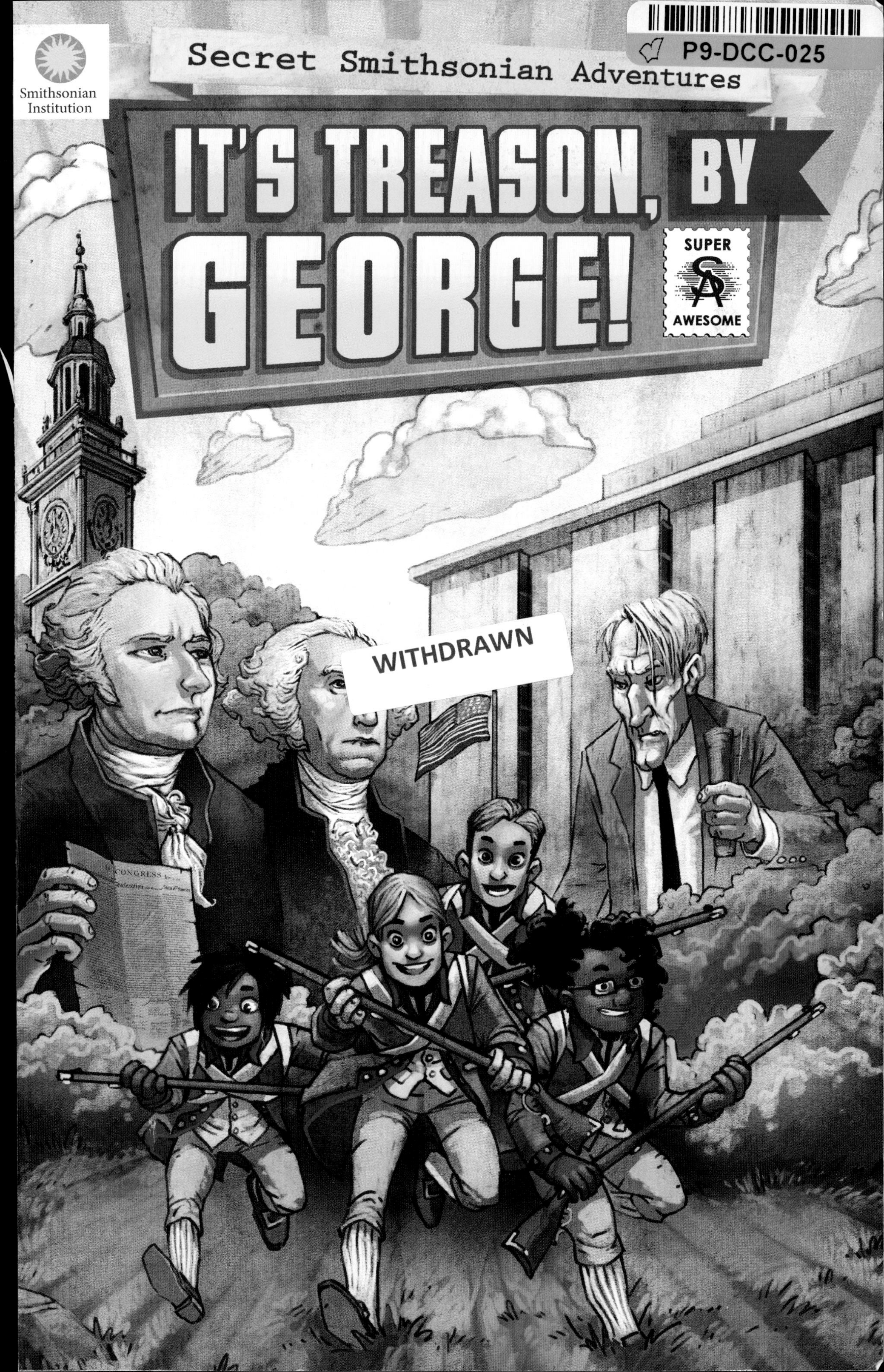
Smithsonian Institution
Secret Smithsonian Adventures
IT'S TREASON, BY GEORGE!
SUPER SA AWESOME
CONGRESS

Secret Smithsonian Adventures

IT'S TREASON, BY GEORGE!

Story by
Steve Hockensmith and Chris Kientz

Illustration by
Lee Nielsen

Color by
Lee Nielsen

Assistant Colorist
Keil Hunka

Lettering by
Dalaney LaGrange

Page Layouts
Andrew Leung

Original Research by
Anthony Bellotti

This book may be purchased for educational, business, or sales promotional use.
For information, please write: Special Markets Department,
Smithsonian Books, P. O. Box 37012, MRC 513, Washington, DC 20013

Published by Smithsonian Books
Director: Carolyn Gleason
Senior Editor: Christina Wiginton
Consulting Curators: Mary Elliott, National Museum of African American History and Culture
Harry Rubenstein, National Museum of American History
Library of Congress Cataloging-in-Publication Data is available upon request.
Manufactured in the United States of America
21 20 19 18 17   5 4 3 2 1

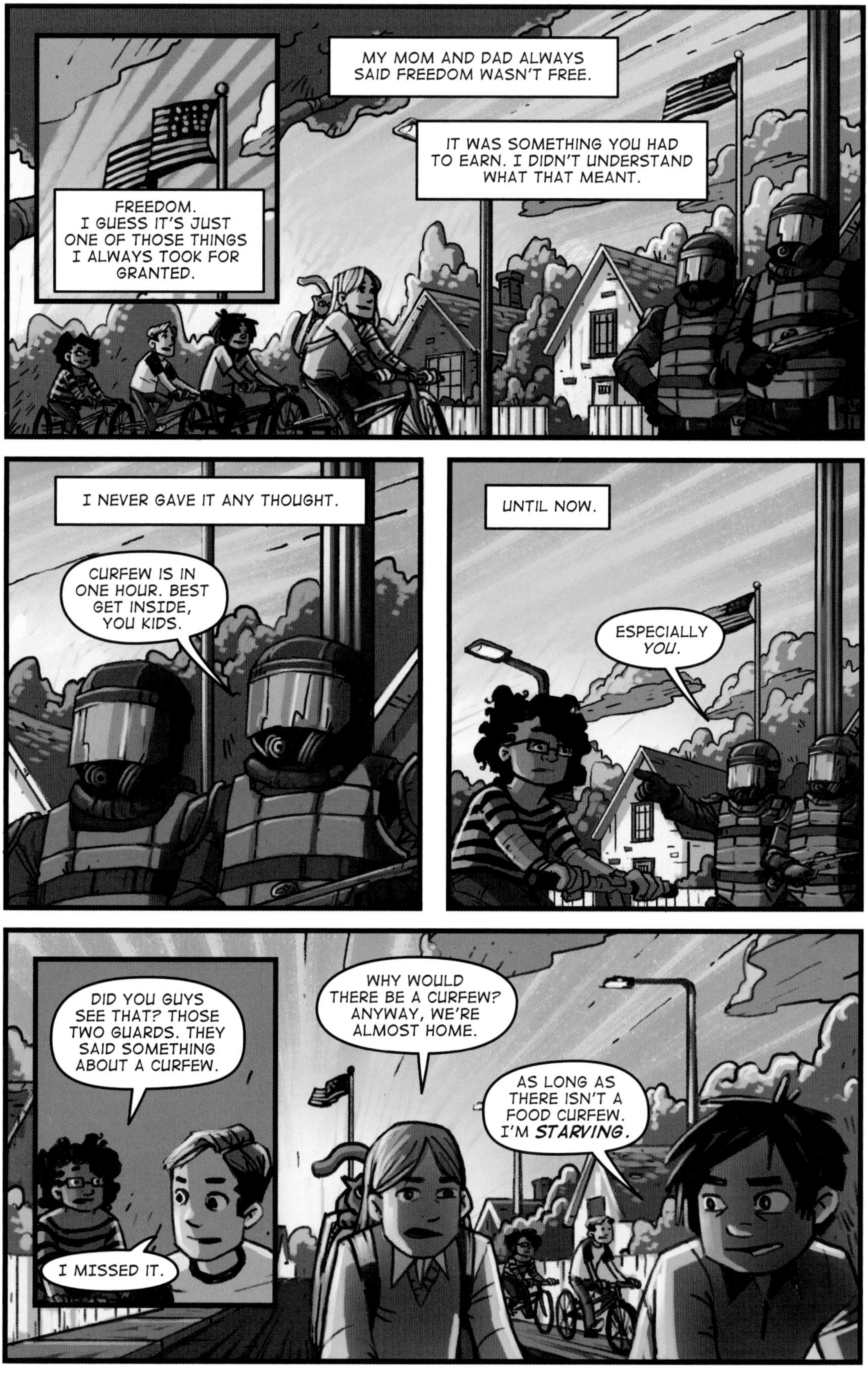
MY MOM AND DAD ALWAYS SAID FREEDOM WASN'T FREE.
IT WAS SOMETHING YOU HAD TO EARN. I DIDN'T UNDERSTAND WHAT THAT MEANT.
FREEDOM. I GUESS IT'S JUST ONE OF THOSE THINGS I ALWAYS TOOK FOR GRANTED.
I NEVER GAVE IT ANY THOUGHT.
CURFEW IS IN ONE HOUR. BEST GET INSIDE, YOU KIDS.
UNTIL NOW.
ESPECIALLY *YOU.*
DID YOU GUYS SEE THAT? THOSE TWO GUARDS. THEY SAID SOMETHING ABOUT A CURFEW.
I MISSED IT.
WHY WOULD THERE BE A CURFEW? ANYWAY, WE'RE ALMOST HOME.
AS LONG AS THERE ISN'T A FOOD CURFEW. I'M ***STARVING.***

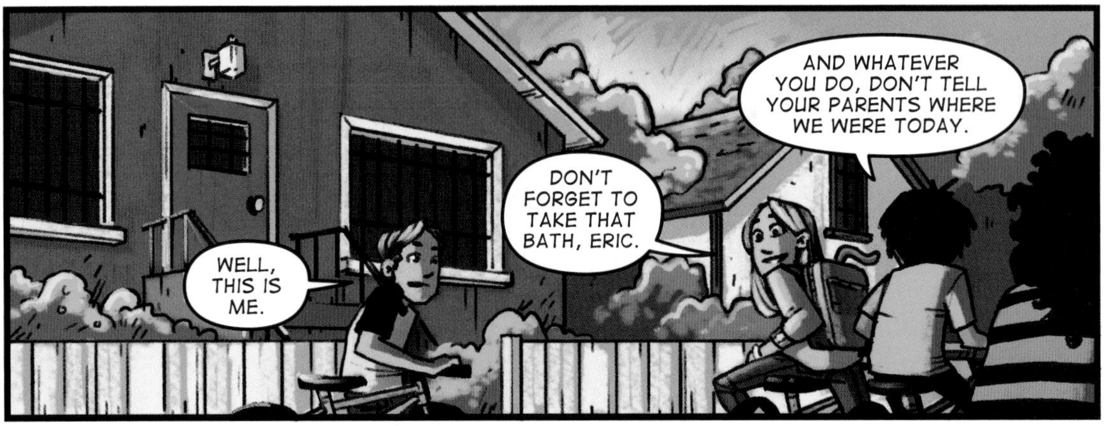
WELL, THIS IS ME.
DON'T FORGET TO TAKE THAT BATH, ERIC.
AND WHATEVER YOU DO, DON'T TELL YOUR PARENTS WHERE WE WERE TODAY.

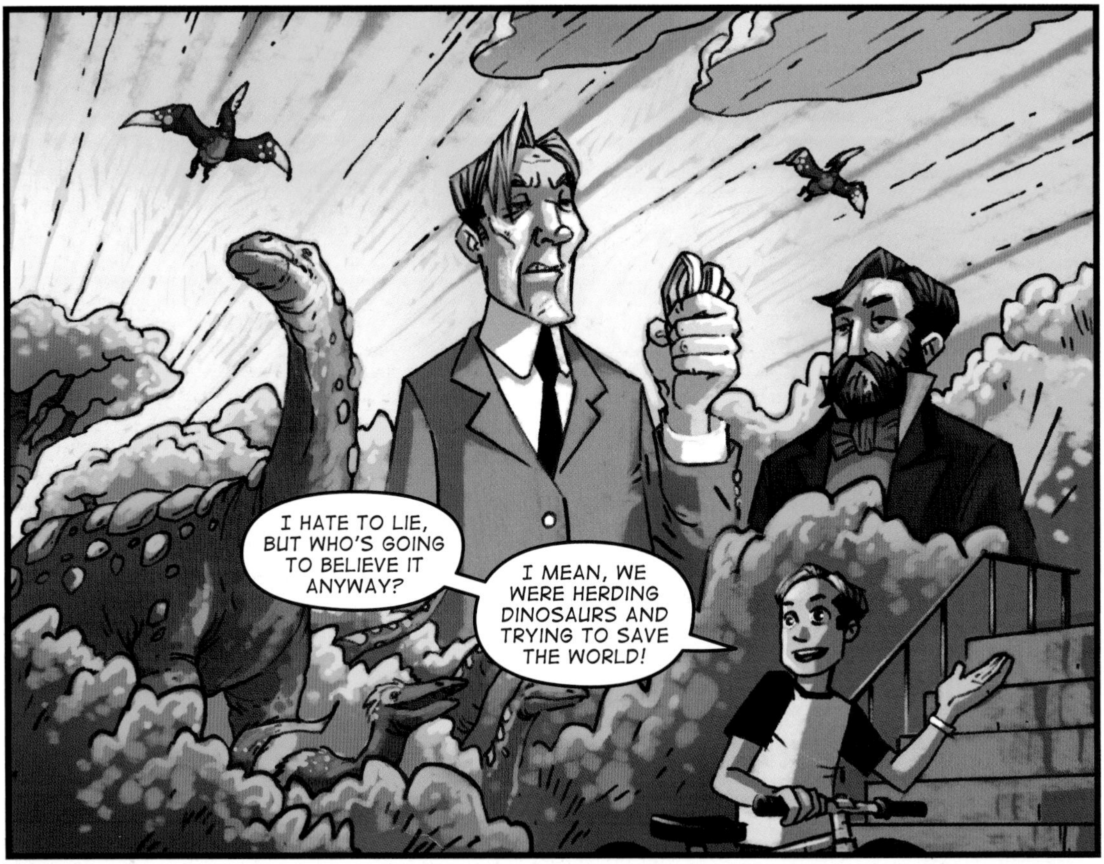
I HATE TO LIE, BUT WHO'S GOING TO BELIEVE IT ANYWAY?
I MEAN, WE WERE HERDING DINOSAURS AND TRYING TO SAVE THE WORLD!

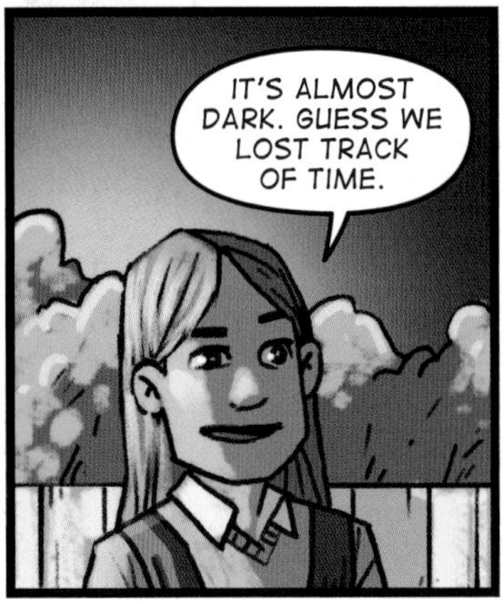
IT'S ALMOST DARK. GUESS WE LOST TRACK OF TIME.

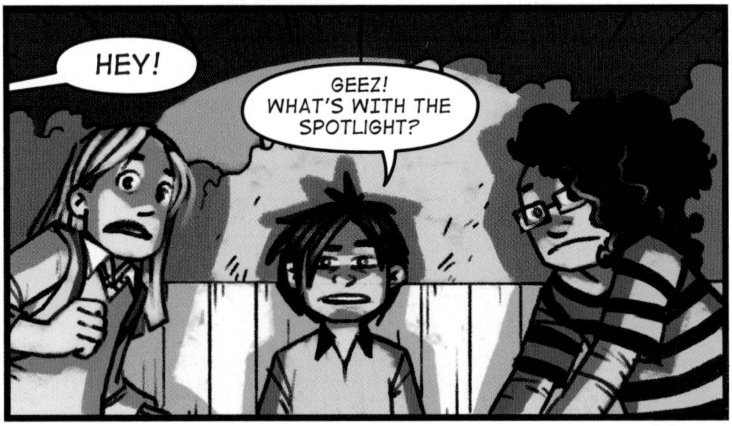
HEY!
GEEZ! WHAT'S WITH THE SPOTLIGHT?

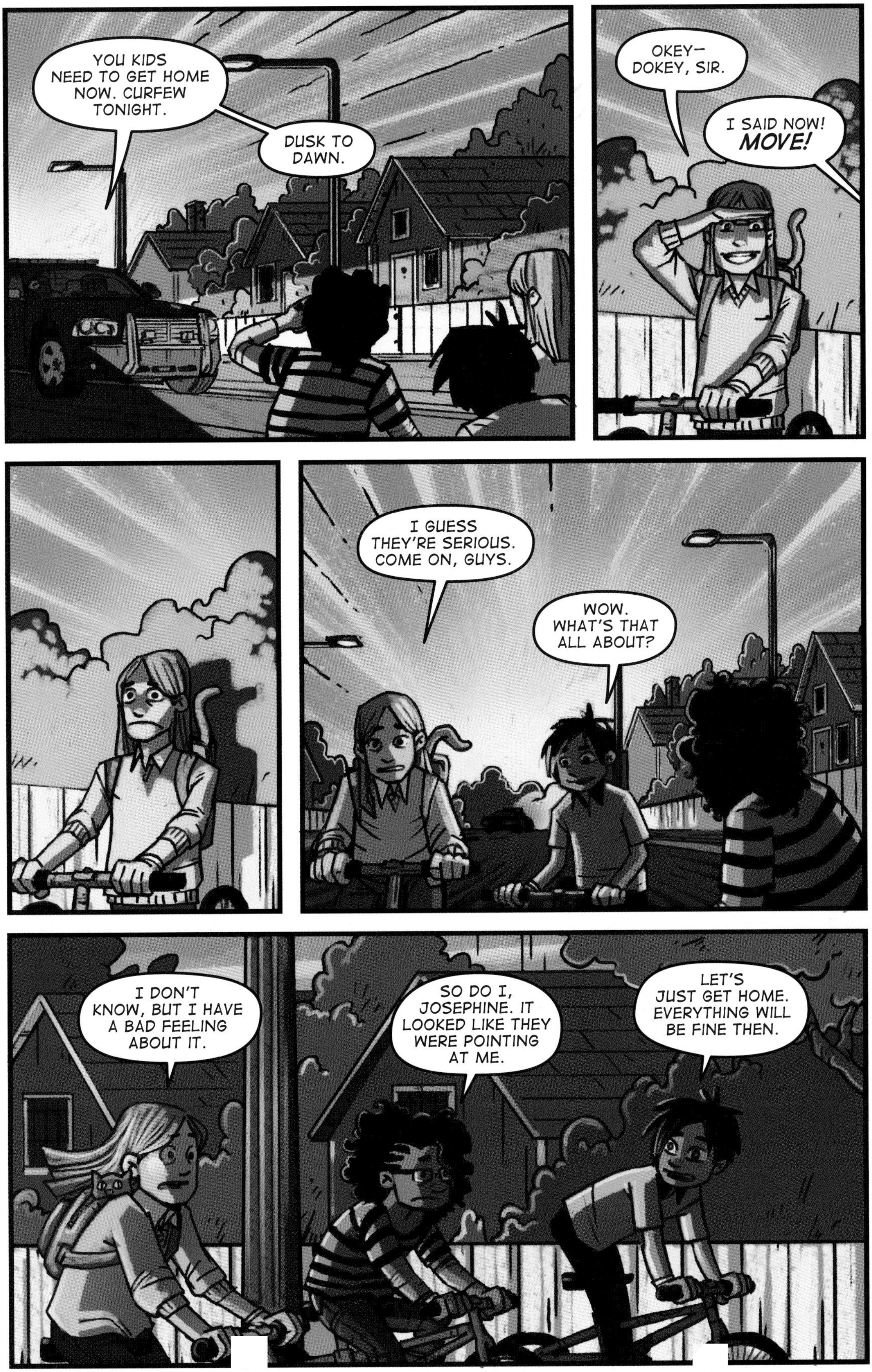
YOU KIDS NEED TO GET HOME NOW. CURFEW TONIGHT.
DUSK TO DAWN.
OKEY-DOKEY, SIR.
I SAID NOW! **MOVE!**
I GUESS THEY'RE SERIOUS. COME ON, GUYS.
WOW. WHAT'S THAT ALL ABOUT?
I DON'T KNOW, BUT I HAVE A BAD FEELING ABOUT IT.
SO DO I, JOSEPHINE. IT LOOKED LIKE THEY WERE POINTING AT ME.
LET'S JUST GET HOME. EVERYTHING WILL BE FINE THEN.

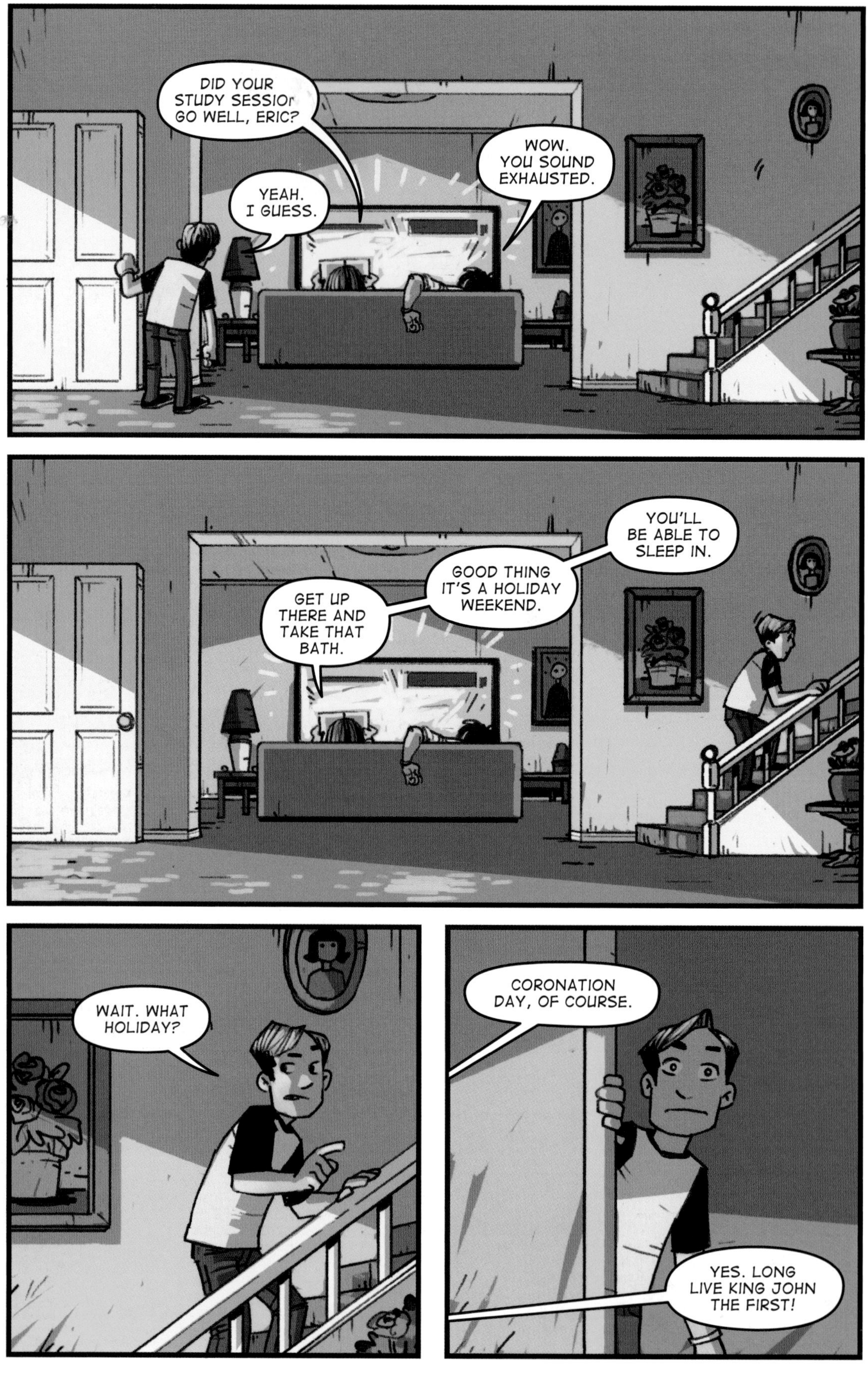
DID YOUR STUDY SESSION GO WELL, ERIC?
YEAH. I GUESS.
WOW. YOU SOUND EXHAUSTED.
GET UP THERE AND TAKE THAT BATH.
GOOD THING IT'S A HOLIDAY WEEKEND.
YOU'LL BE ABLE TO SLEEP IN.
WAIT. WHAT HOLIDAY?
CORONATION DAY, OF COURSE.
YES. LONG LIVE KING JOHN THE FIRST!

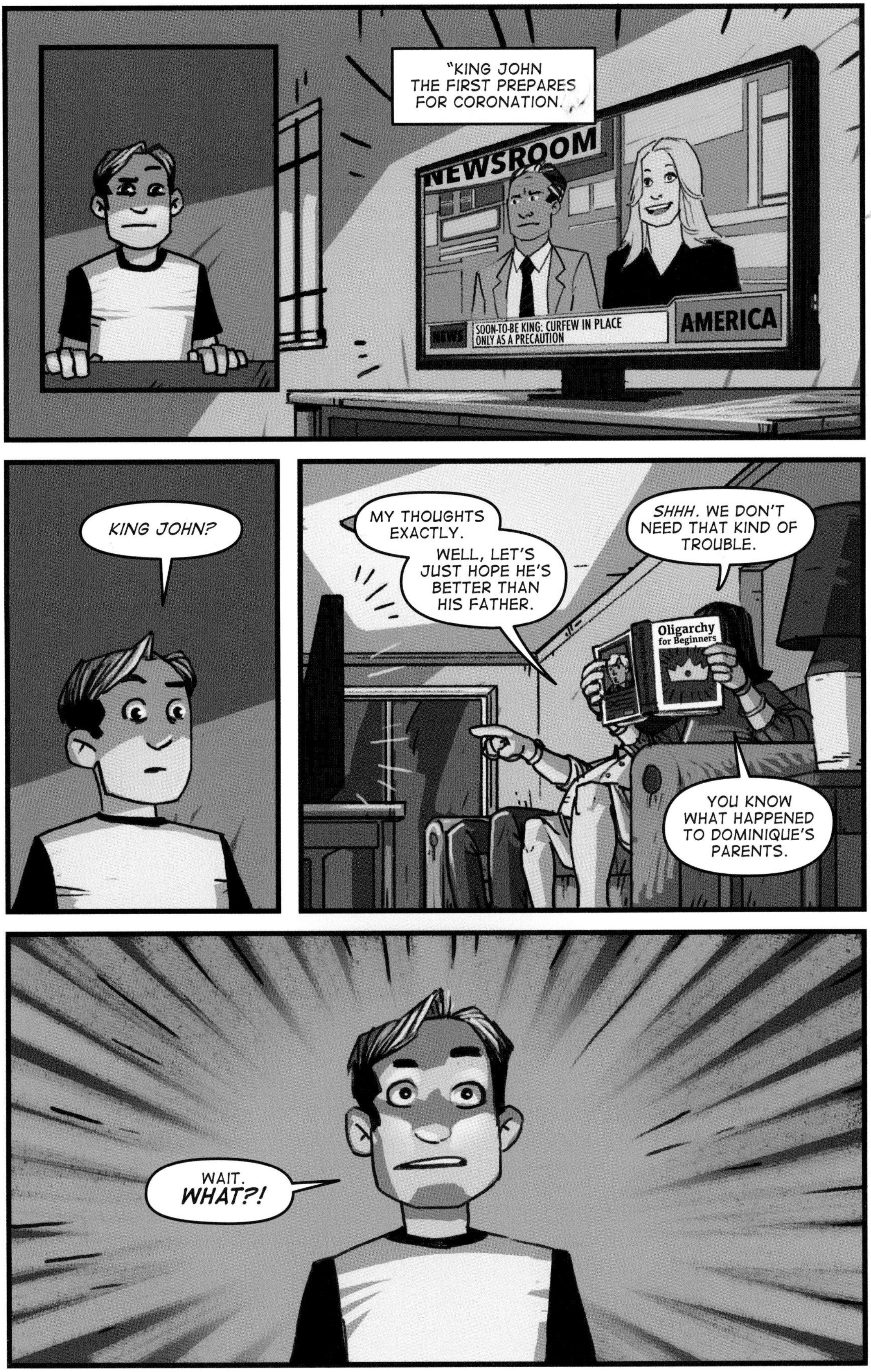
"KING JOHN THE FIRST PREPARES FOR CORONATION.
NEWSROOM
NEWS
SOON-TO-BE KING: CURFEW IN PLACE ONLY AS A PRECAUTION
AMERICA
KING JOHN?
MY THOUGHTS EXACTLY.
WELL, LET'S JUST HOPE HE'S BETTER THAN HIS FATHER.
SHHH. WE DON'T NEED THAT KIND OF TROUBLE.
Oligarchy for Beginners
YOU KNOW WHAT HAPPENED TO DOMINIQUE'S PARENTS.
WAIT. WHAT?!

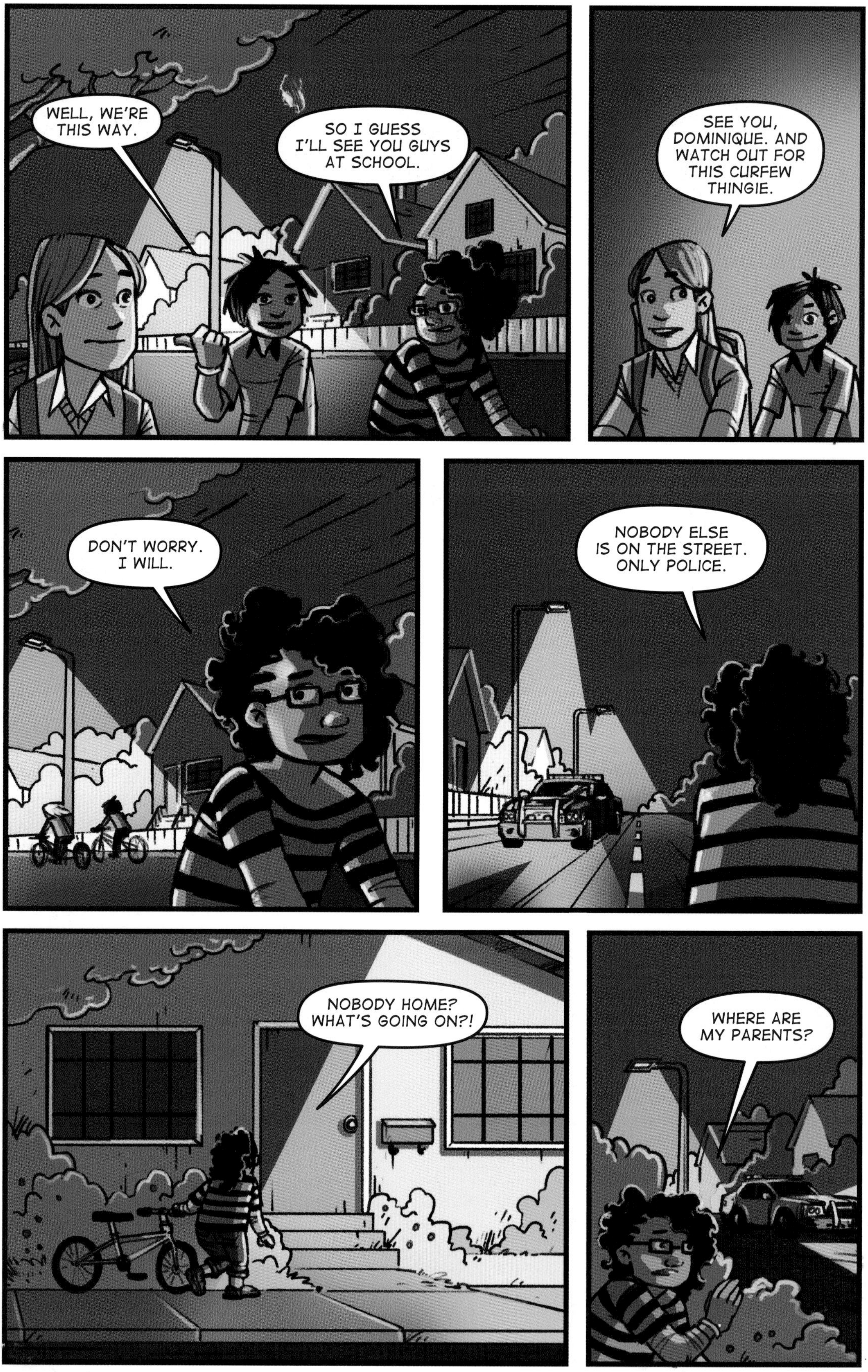
WELL, WE'RE THIS WAY.
SO I GUESS I'LL SEE YOU GUYS AT SCHOOL.
SEE YOU, DOMINIQUE. AND WATCH OUT FOR THIS CURFEW THINGIE.
DON'T WORRY. I WILL.
NOBODY ELSE IS ON THE STREET. ONLY POLICE.
NOBODY HOME? WHAT'S GOING ON?!
WHERE ARE MY PARENTS?

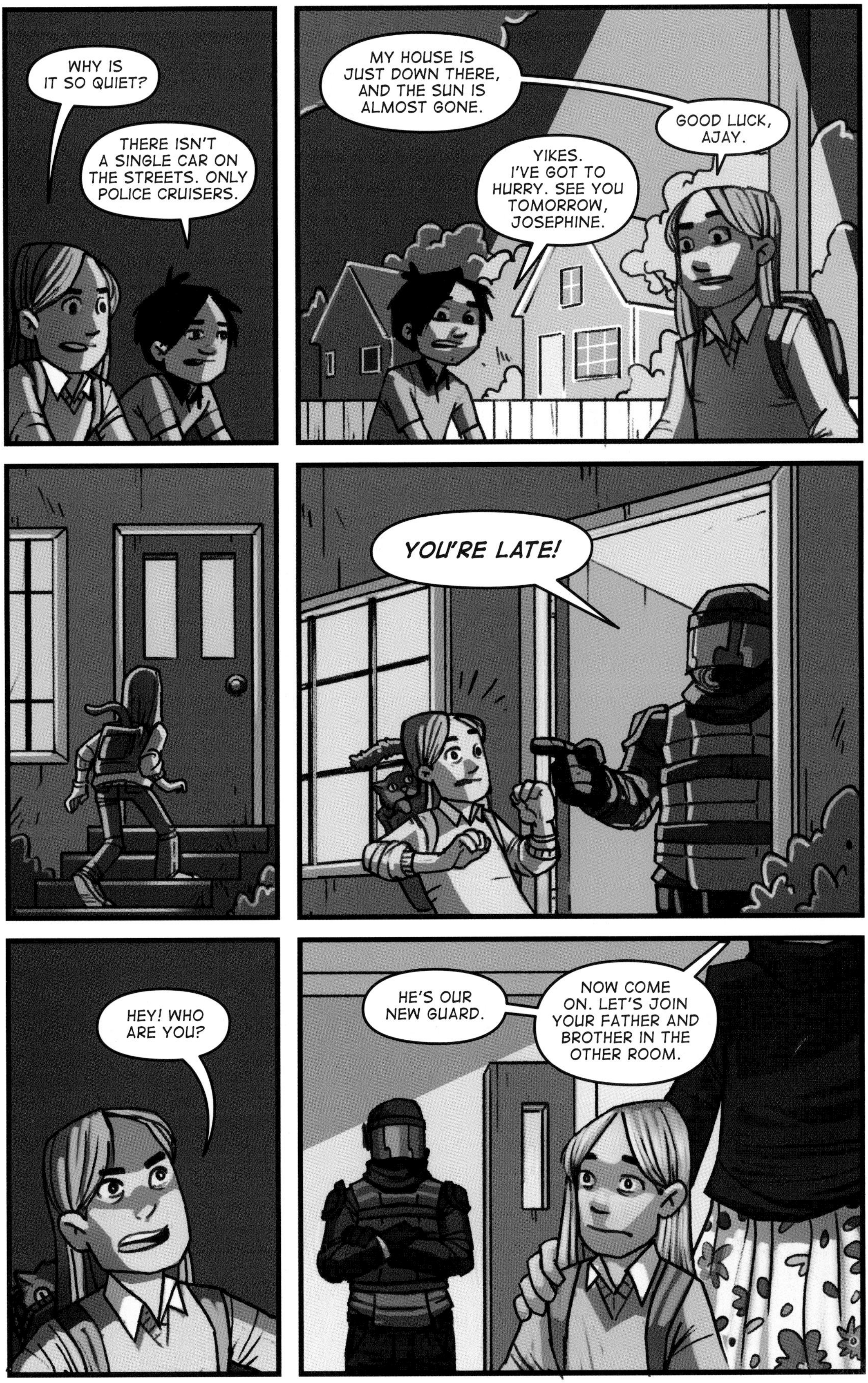
WHY IS IT SO QUIET?
THERE ISN'T A SINGLE CAR ON THE STREETS. ONLY POLICE CRUISERS.
MY HOUSE IS JUST DOWN THERE, AND THE SUN IS ALMOST GONE.
GOOD LUCK, AJAY.
YIKES. I'VE GOT TO HURRY. SEE YOU TOMORROW, JOSEPHINE.
YOU'RE LATE!
HEY! WHO ARE YOU?
HE'S OUR NEW GUARD.
NOW COME ON. LET'S JOIN YOUR FATHER AND BROTHER IN THE OTHER ROOM.

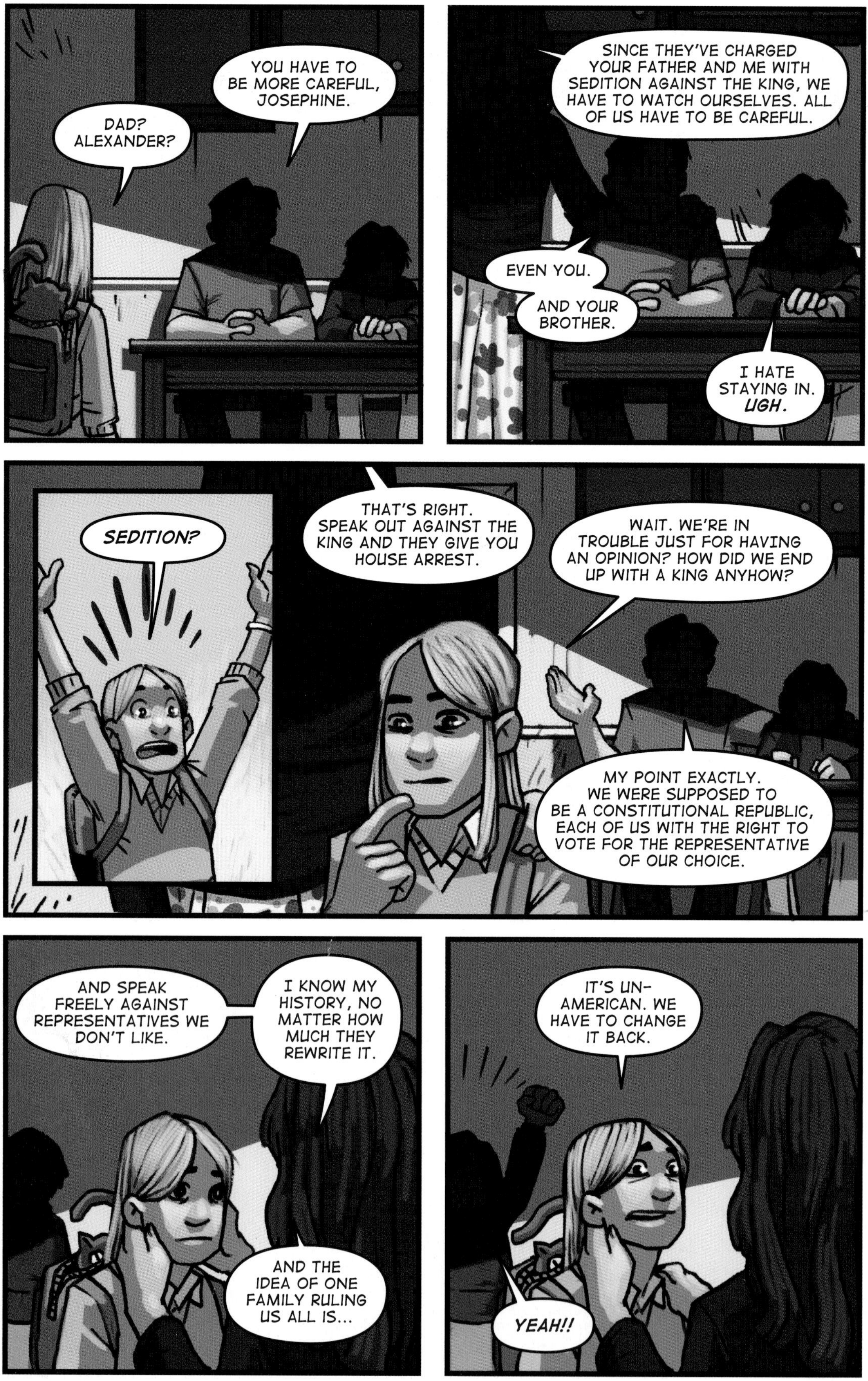
DAD? ALEXANDER?
YOU HAVE TO BE MORE CAREFUL, JOSEPHINE.
SINCE THEY'VE CHARGED YOUR FATHER AND ME WITH SEDITION AGAINST THE KING, WE HAVE TO WATCH OURSELVES. ALL OF US HAVE TO BE CAREFUL.
EVEN YOU.
AND YOUR BROTHER.
I HATE STAYING IN. UGH.
SEDITION?
THAT'S RIGHT. SPEAK OUT AGAINST THE KING AND THEY GIVE YOU HOUSE ARREST.
WAIT. WE'RE IN TROUBLE JUST FOR HAVING AN OPINION? HOW DID WE END UP WITH A KING ANYHOW?
MY POINT EXACTLY. WE WERE SUPPOSED TO BE A CONSTITUTIONAL REPUBLIC, EACH OF US WITH THE RIGHT TO VOTE FOR THE REPRESENTATIVE OF OUR CHOICE.
AND SPEAK FREELY AGAINST REPRESENTATIVES WE DON'T LIKE.
I KNOW MY HISTORY, NO MATTER HOW MUCH THEY REWRITE IT.
AND THE IDEA OF ONE FAMILY RULING US ALL IS...
IT'S UN-AMERICAN. WE HAVE TO CHANGE IT BACK.
YEAH!!

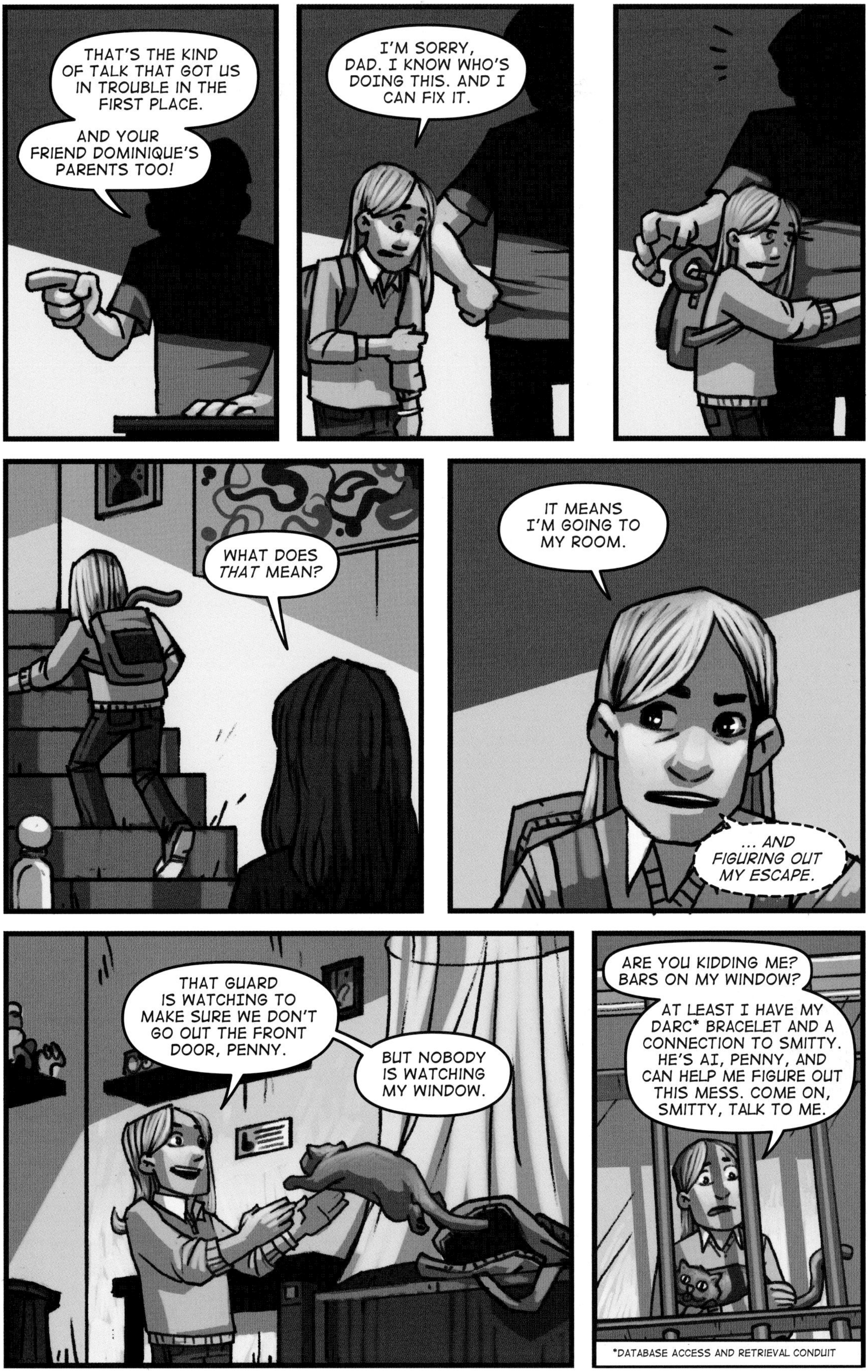
THAT'S THE KIND OF TALK THAT GOT US IN TROUBLE IN THE FIRST PLACE.
AND YOUR FRIEND DOMINIQUE'S PARENTS TOO!
I'M SORRY, DAD. I KNOW WHO'S DOING THIS. AND I CAN FIX IT.
WHAT DOES *THAT* MEAN?
IT MEANS I'M GOING TO MY ROOM.
... AND FIGURING OUT MY ESCAPE.
THAT GUARD IS WATCHING TO MAKE SURE WE DON'T GO OUT THE FRONT DOOR, PENNY.
BUT NOBODY IS WATCHING MY WINDOW.
ARE YOU KIDDING ME? BARS ON MY WINDOW?
AT LEAST I HAVE MY DARC* BRACELET AND A CONNECTION TO SMITTY. HE'S AI, PENNY, AND CAN HELP ME FIGURE OUT THIS MESS. COME ON, SMITTY, TALK TO ME.
*DATABASE ACCESS AND RETRIEVAL CONDUIT

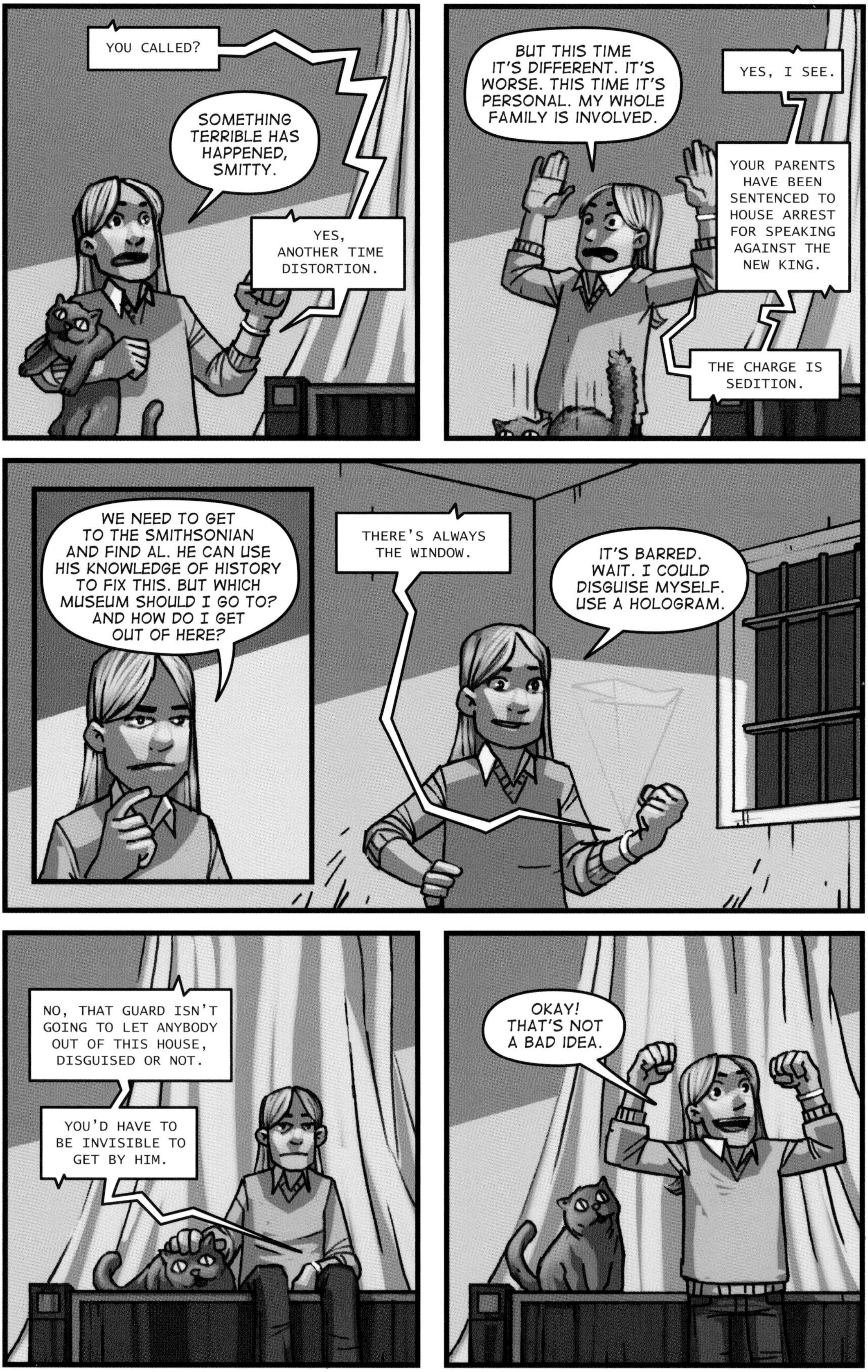
YOU CALLED?
SOMETHING TERRIBLE HAS HAPPENED, SMITTY.
YES, ANOTHER TIME DISTORTION.
BUT THIS TIME IT'S DIFFERENT. IT'S WORSE. THIS TIME IT'S PERSONAL. MY WHOLE FAMILY IS INVOLVED.
YES, I SEE.
YOUR PARENTS HAVE BEEN SENTENCED TO HOUSE ARREST FOR SPEAKING AGAINST THE NEW KING.
THE CHARGE IS SEDITION.
WE NEED TO GET TO THE SMITHSONIAN AND FIND AL. HE CAN USE HIS KNOWLEDGE OF HISTORY TO FIX THIS. BUT WHICH MUSEUM SHOULD I GO TO? AND HOW DO I GET OUT OF HERE?
THERE'S ALWAYS THE WINDOW.
IT'S BARRED. WAIT. I COULD DISGUISE MYSELF. USE A HOLOGRAM.
NO, THAT GUARD ISN'T GOING TO LET ANYBODY OUT OF THIS HOUSE, DISGUISED OR NOT.
YOU'D HAVE TO BE INVISIBLE TO GET BY HIM.
OKAY! THAT'S NOT A BAD IDEA.

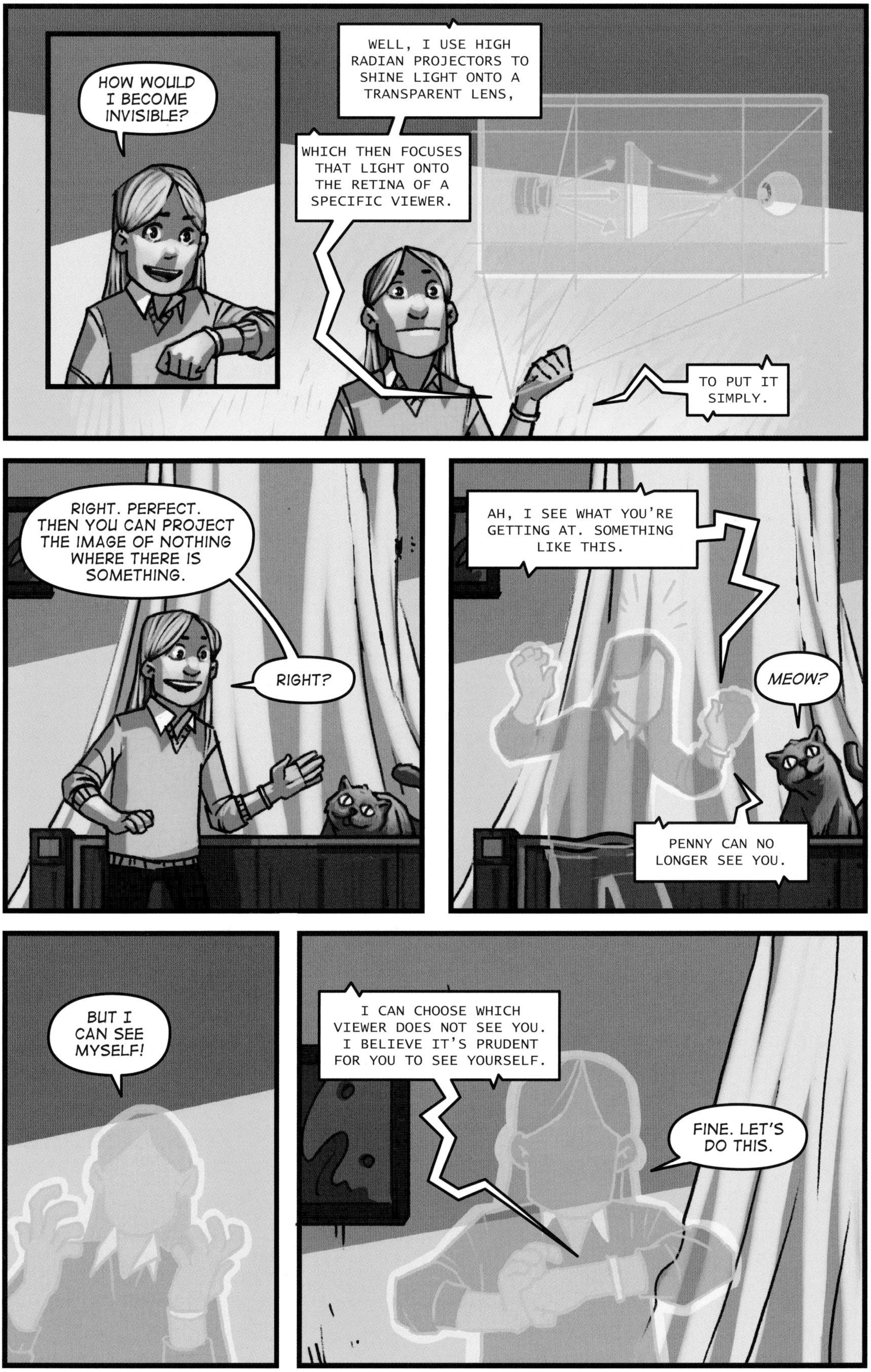
HOW WOULD I BECOME INVISIBLE?
WELL, I USE HIGH RADIAN PROJECTORS TO SHINE LIGHT ONTO A TRANSPARENT LENS,
WHICH THEN FOCUSES THAT LIGHT ONTO THE RETINA OF A SPECIFIC VIEWER.
TO PUT IT SIMPLY.
RIGHT. PERFECT. THEN YOU CAN PROJECT THE IMAGE OF NOTHING WHERE THERE IS SOMETHING.
RIGHT?
AH, I SEE WHAT YOU'RE GETTING AT. SOMETHING LIKE THIS.
MEOW?
PENNY CAN NO LONGER SEE YOU.
BUT I CAN SEE MYSELF!
I CAN CHOOSE WHICH VIEWER DOES NOT SEE YOU. I BELIEVE IT'S PRUDENT FOR YOU TO SEE YOURSELF.
FINE. LET'S DO THIS.

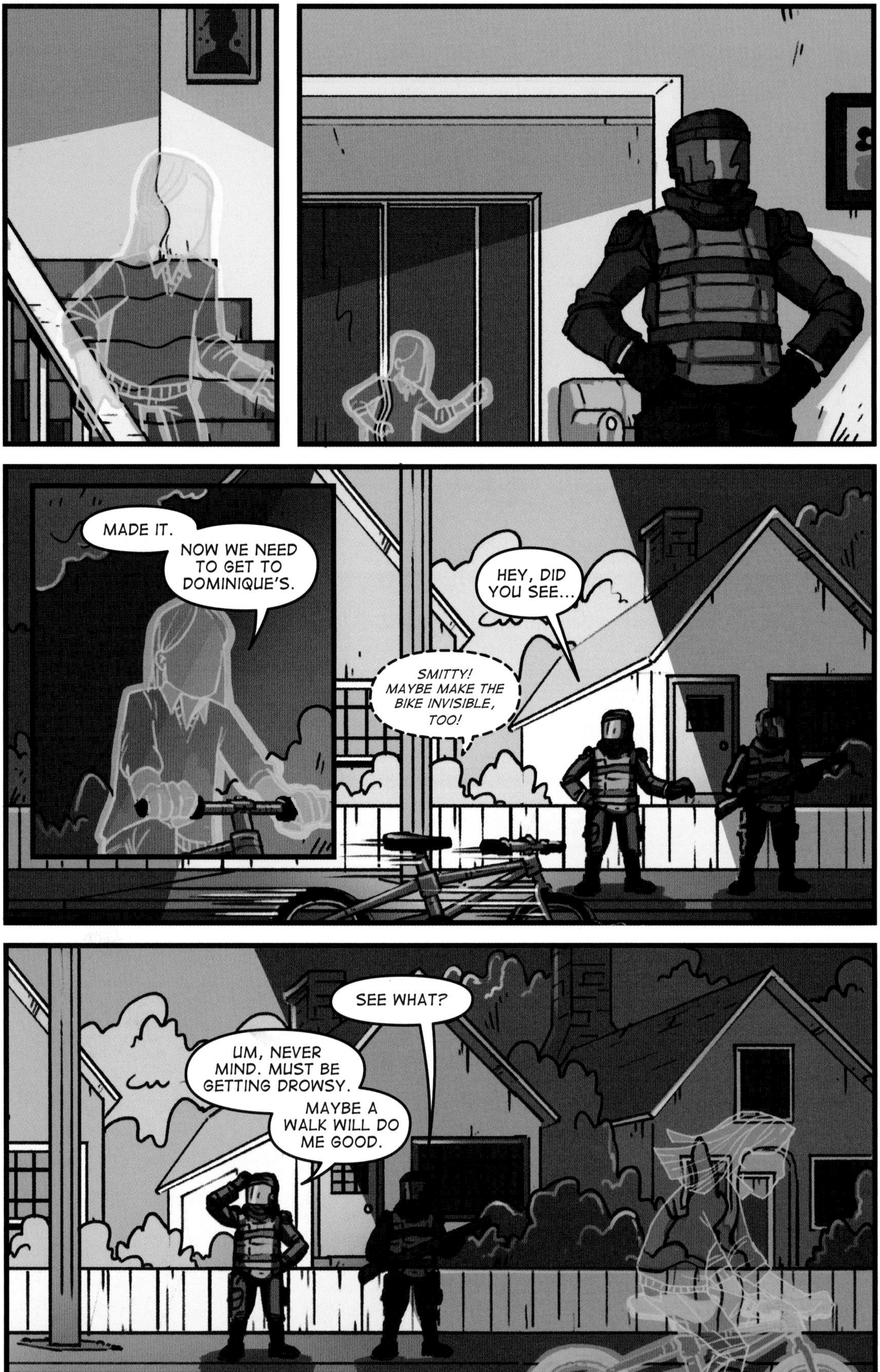
MADE IT.
NOW WE NEED TO GET TO DOMINIQUE'S.
HEY, DID YOU SEE...
SMITTY! MAYBE MAKE THE BIKE INVISIBLE, TOO!
SEE WHAT?
UM, NEVER MIND. MUST BE GETTING DROWSY.
MAYBE A WALK WILL DO ME GOOD.

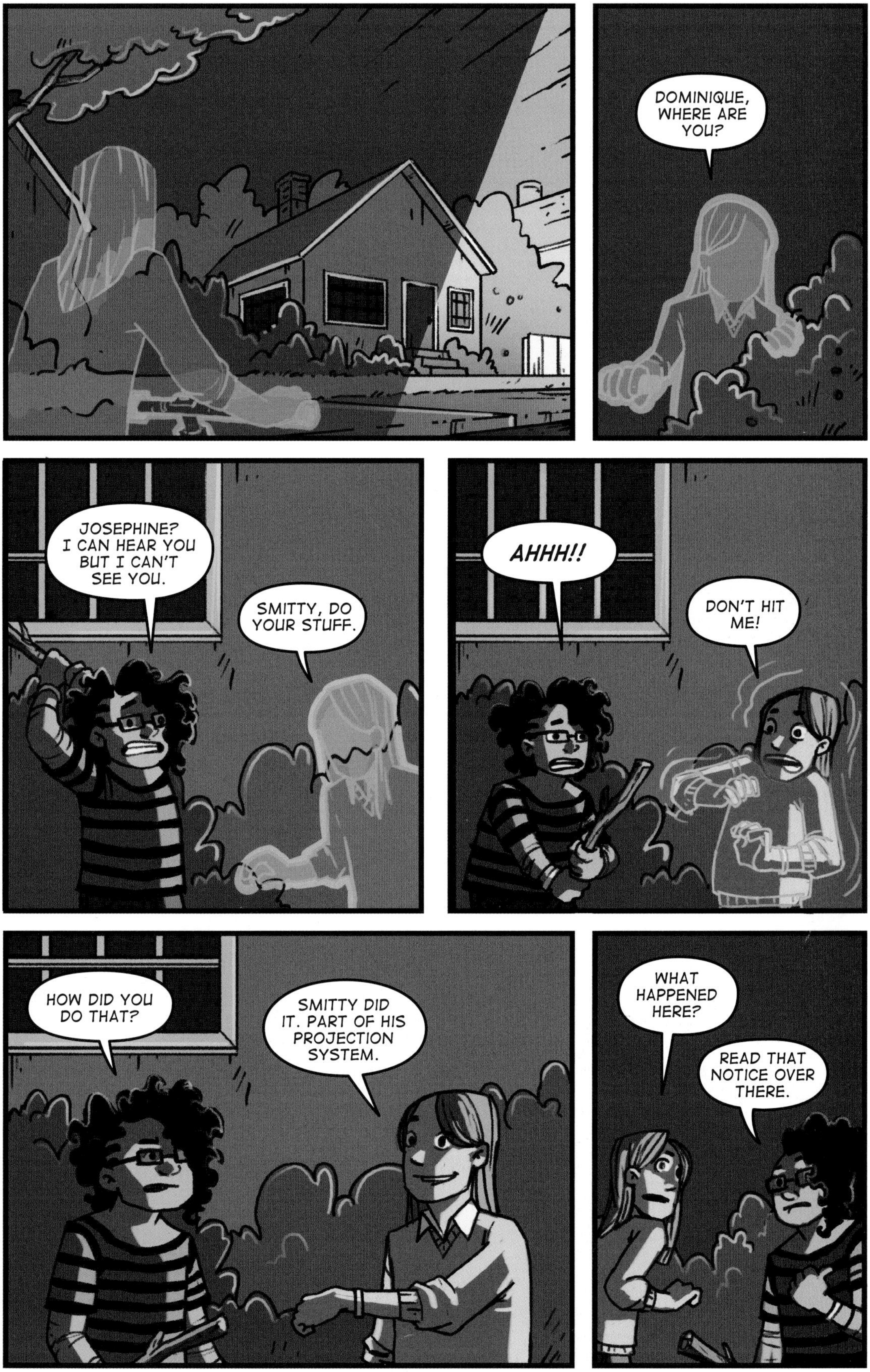
DOMINIQUE, WHERE ARE YOU?
JOSEPHINE? I CAN HEAR YOU BUT I CAN'T SEE YOU.
SMITTY, DO YOUR STUFF.
AHHH!!
DON'T HIT ME!
HOW DID YOU DO THAT?
SMITTY DID IT. PART OF HIS PROJECTION SYSTEM.
WHAT HAPPENED HERE?
READ THAT NOTICE OVER THERE.

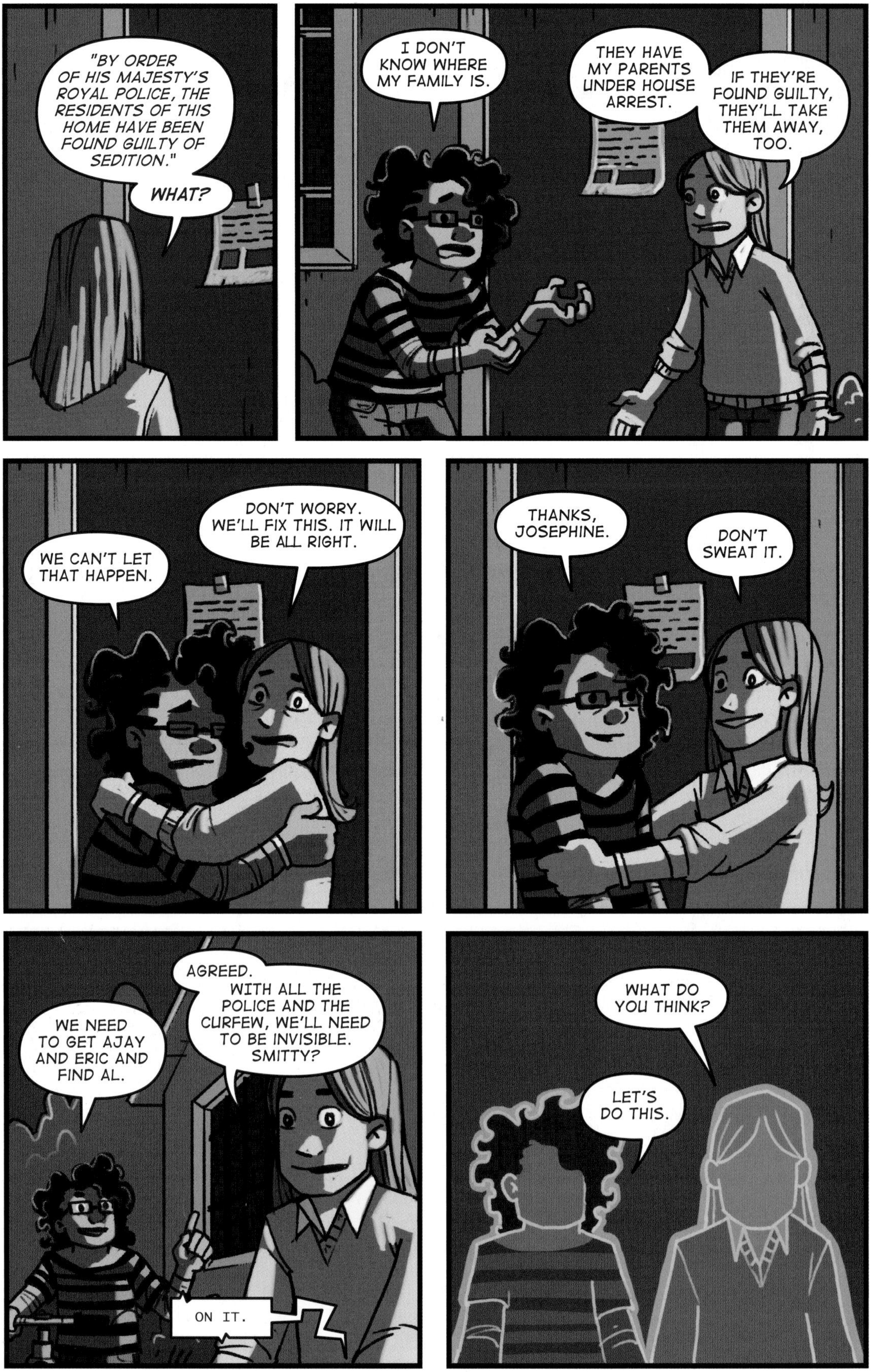
"BY ORDER OF HIS MAJESTY'S ROYAL POLICE, THE RESIDENTS OF THIS HOME HAVE BEEN FOUND GUILTY OF SEDITION."
WHAT?
I DON'T KNOW WHERE MY FAMILY IS.
THEY HAVE MY PARENTS UNDER HOUSE ARREST.
IF THEY'RE FOUND GUILTY, THEY'LL TAKE THEM AWAY, TOO.
WE CAN'T LET THAT HAPPEN.
DON'T WORRY. WE'LL FIX THIS. IT WILL BE ALL RIGHT.
THANKS, JOSEPHINE.
DON'T SWEAT IT.
WE NEED TO GET AJAY AND ERIC AND FIND AL.
AGREED. WITH ALL THE POLICE AND THE CURFEW, WE'LL NEED TO BE INVISIBLE. SMITTY?
ON IT.
WHAT DO YOU THINK?
LET'S DO THIS.

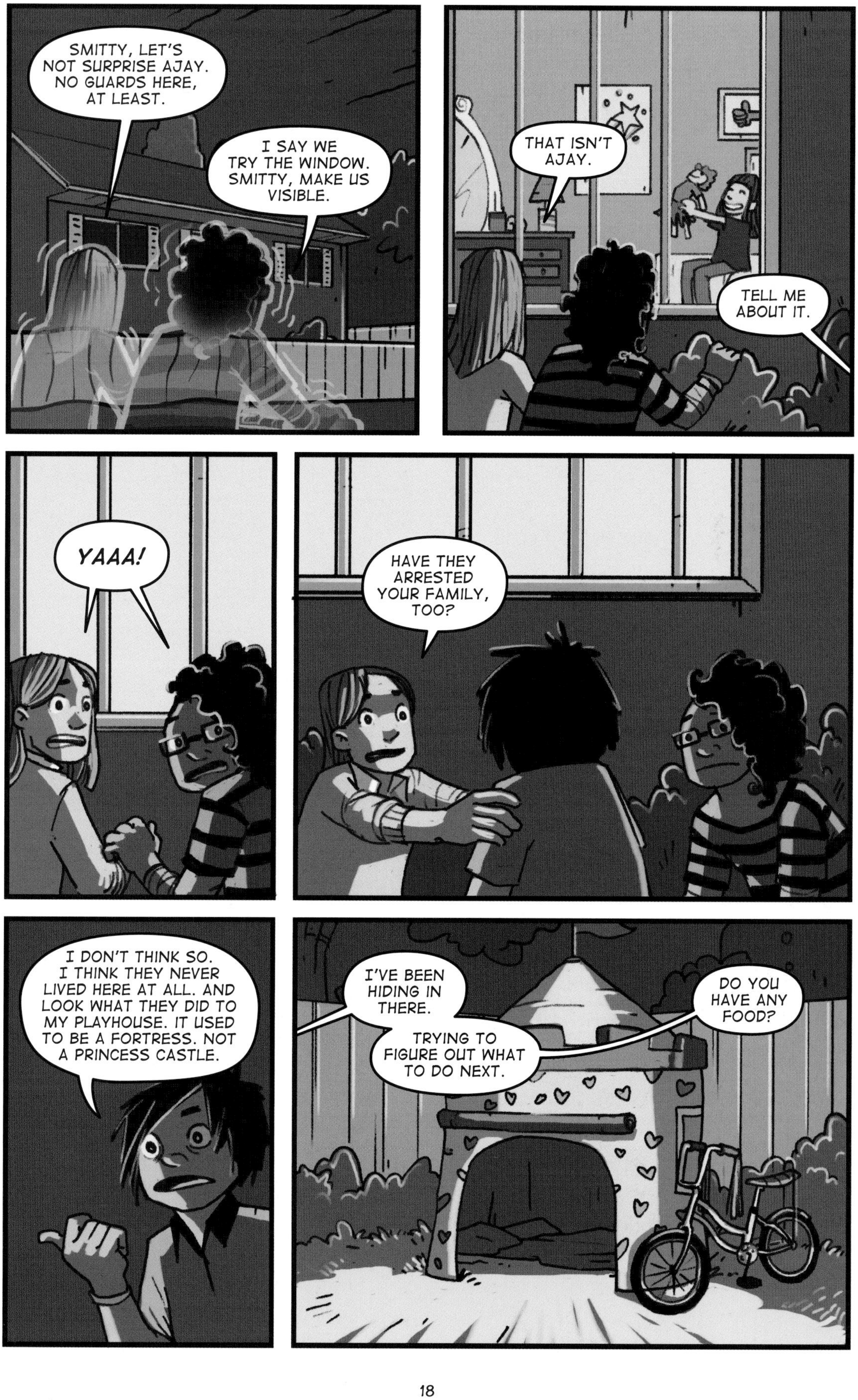
SMITTY, LET'S NOT SURPRISE AJAY. NO GUARDS HERE, AT LEAST.
I SAY WE TRY THE WINDOW. SMITTY, MAKE US VISIBLE.
THAT ISN'T AJAY.
TELL ME ABOUT IT.
YAAA!
HAVE THEY ARRESTED YOUR FAMILY, TOO?
I DON'T THINK SO. I THINK THEY NEVER LIVED HERE AT ALL. AND LOOK WHAT THEY DID TO MY PLAYHOUSE. IT USED TO BE A FORTRESS. NOT A PRINCESS CASTLE.
I'VE BEEN HIDING IN THERE.
TRYING TO FIGURE OUT WHAT TO DO NEXT.
DO YOU HAVE ANY FOOD?

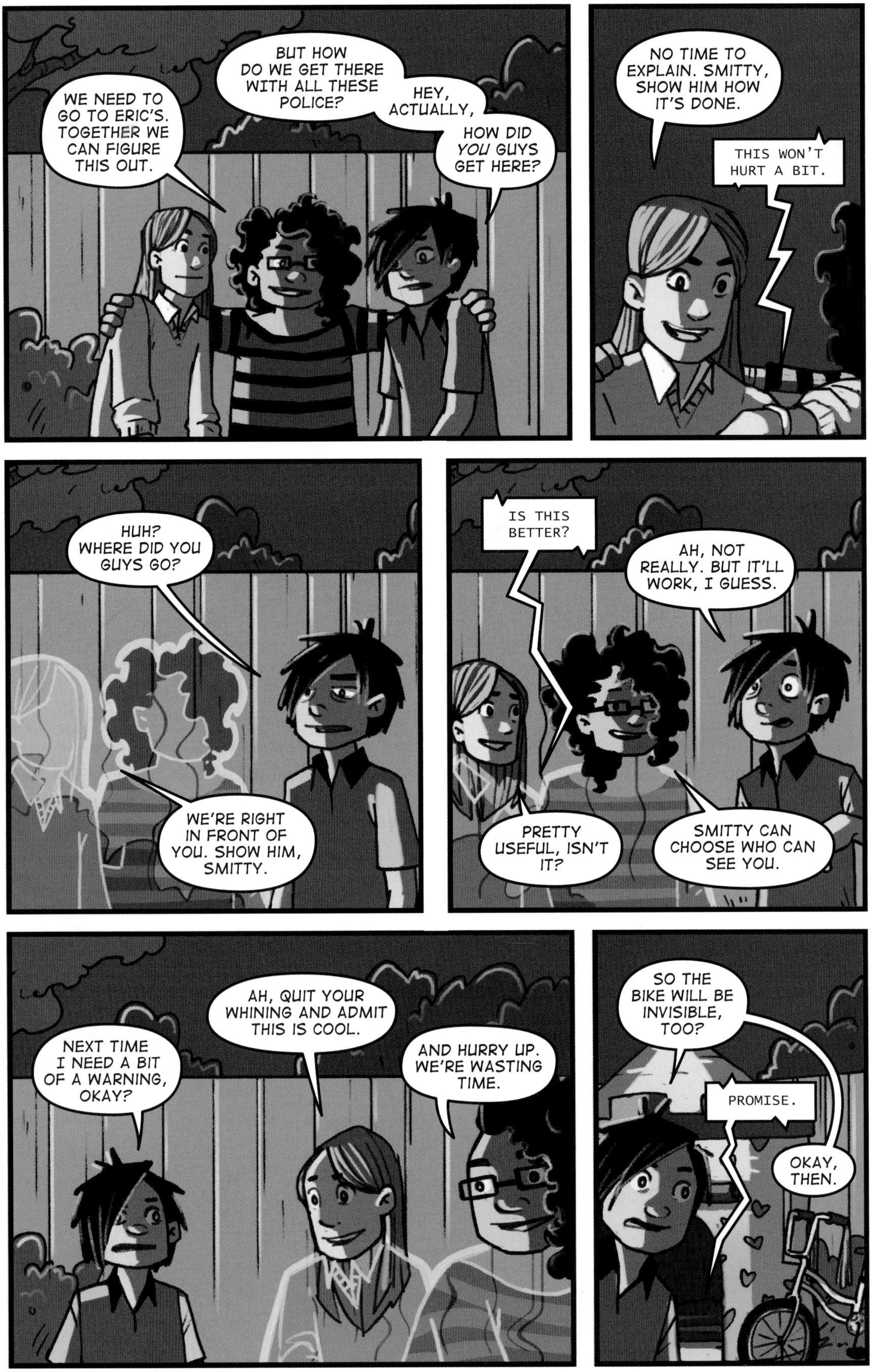
WE NEED TO GO TO ERIC'S. TOGETHER WE CAN FIGURE THIS OUT.
BUT HOW DO WE GET THERE WITH ALL THESE POLICE?
HEY, ACTUALLY,
HOW DID *YOU* GUYS GET HERE?
NO TIME TO EXPLAIN. SMITTY, SHOW HIM HOW IT'S DONE.
THIS WON'T HURT A BIT.
HUH? WHERE DID YOU GUYS GO?
WE'RE RIGHT IN FRONT OF YOU. SHOW HIM, SMITTY.
IS THIS BETTER?
AH, NOT REALLY. BUT IT'LL WORK, I GUESS.
PRETTY USEFUL, ISN'T IT?
SMITTY CAN CHOOSE WHO CAN SEE YOU.
NEXT TIME I NEED A BIT OF A WARNING, OKAY?
AH, QUIT YOUR WHINING AND ADMIT THIS IS COOL.
AND HURRY UP. WE'RE WASTING TIME.
SO THE BIKE WILL BE INVISIBLE, TOO?
PROMISE.
OKAY, THEN.

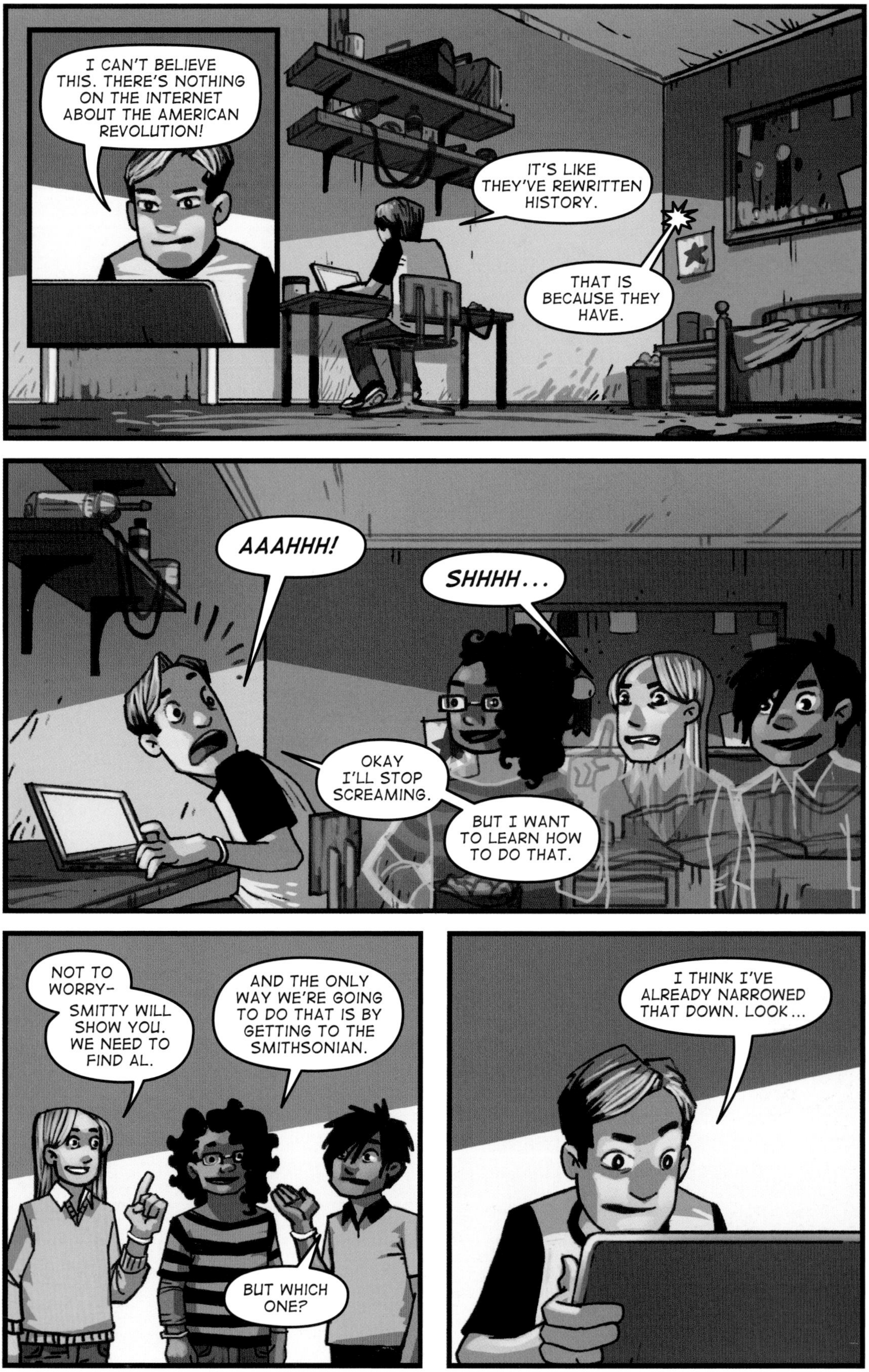
I CAN'T BELIEVE THIS. THERE'S NOTHING ON THE INTERNET ABOUT THE AMERICAN REVOLUTION!
IT'S LIKE THEY'VE REWRITTEN HISTORY.
THAT IS BECAUSE THEY HAVE.
AAAHHH!
SHHHH...
OKAY I'LL STOP SCREAMING.
BUT I WANT TO LEARN HOW TO DO THAT.
NOT TO WORRY-
SMITTY WILL SHOW YOU. WE NEED TO FIND AL.
AND THE ONLY WAY WE'RE GOING TO DO THAT IS BY GETTING TO THE SMITHSONIAN.
BUT WHICH ONE?
I THINK I'VE ALREADY NARROWED THAT DOWN. LOOK...

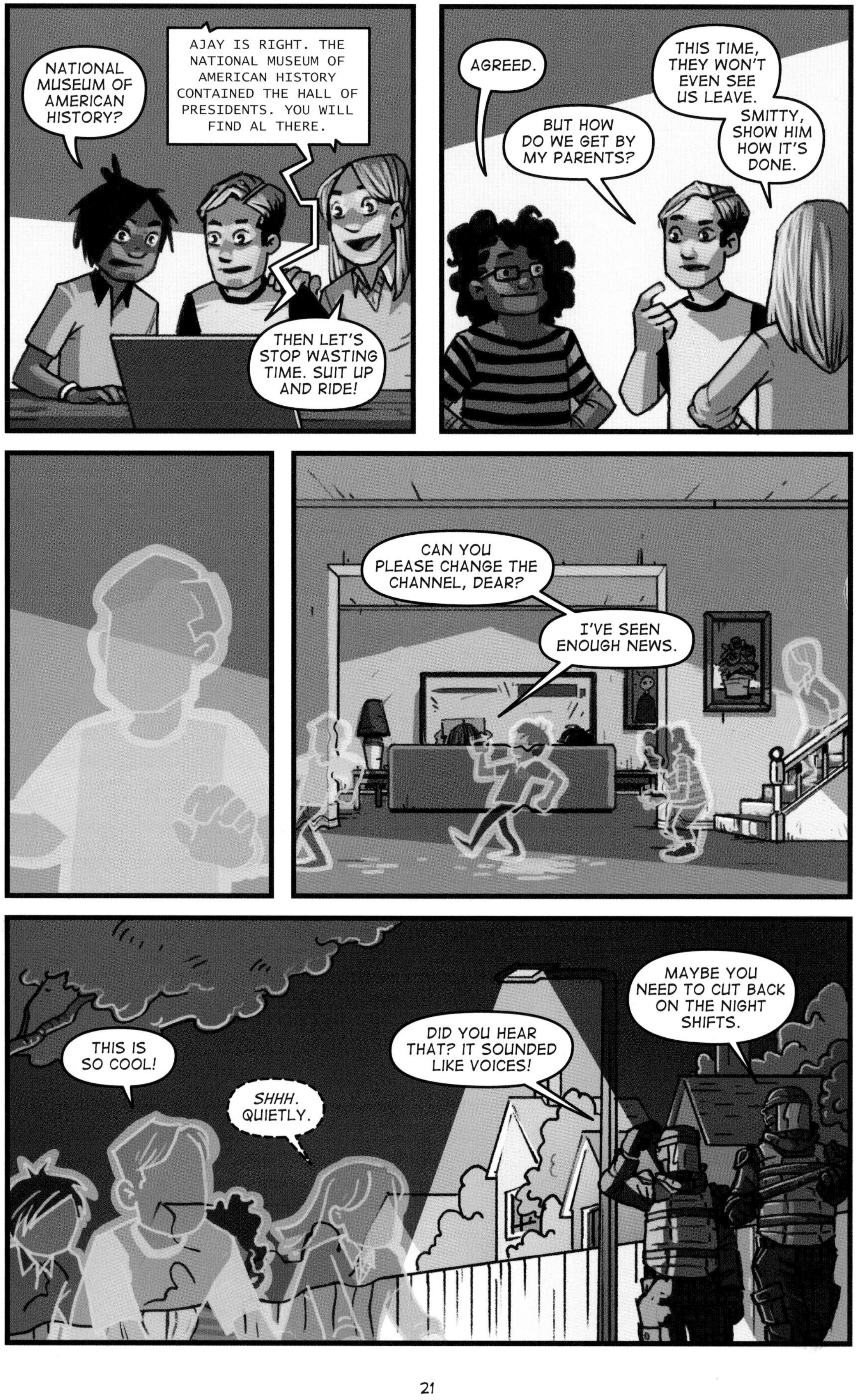
NATIONAL MUSEUM OF AMERICAN HISTORY?
AJAY IS RIGHT. THE NATIONAL MUSEUM OF AMERICAN HISTORY CONTAINED THE HALL OF PRESIDENTS. YOU WILL FIND AL THERE.
THEN LET'S STOP WASTING TIME. SUIT UP AND RIDE!
AGREED.
BUT HOW DO WE GET BY MY PARENTS?
THIS TIME, THEY WON'T EVEN SEE US LEAVE.
SMITTY, SHOW HIM HOW IT'S DONE.
CAN YOU PLEASE CHANGE THE CHANNEL, DEAR?
I'VE SEEN ENOUGH NEWS.
THIS IS SO COOL!
SHHH. QUIETLY.
DID YOU HEAR THAT? IT SOUNDED LIKE VOICES!
MAYBE YOU NEED TO CUT BACK ON THE NIGHT SHIFTS.

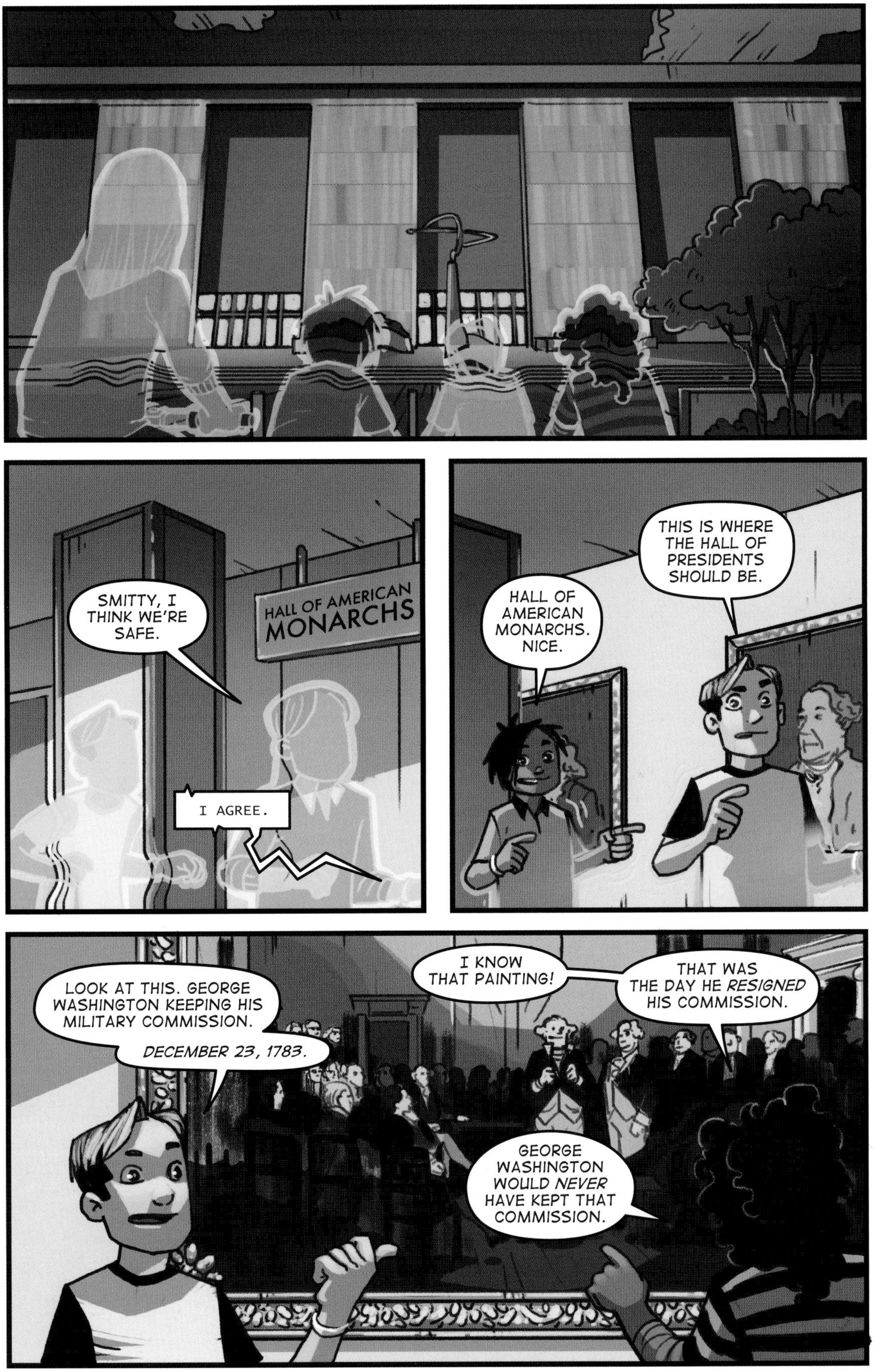
SMITTY, I THINK WE'RE SAFE.
HALL OF AMERICAN MONARCHS
I AGREE.
HALL OF AMERICAN MONARCHS. NICE.
THIS IS WHERE THE HALL OF PRESIDENTS SHOULD BE.
LOOK AT THIS. GEORGE WASHINGTON KEEPING HIS MILITARY COMMISSION.
DECEMBER 23, 1783.
I KNOW THAT PAINTING!
THAT WAS THE DAY HE *RESIGNED* HIS COMMISSION.
GEORGE WASHINGTON WOULD *NEVER* HAVE KEPT THAT COMMISSION.

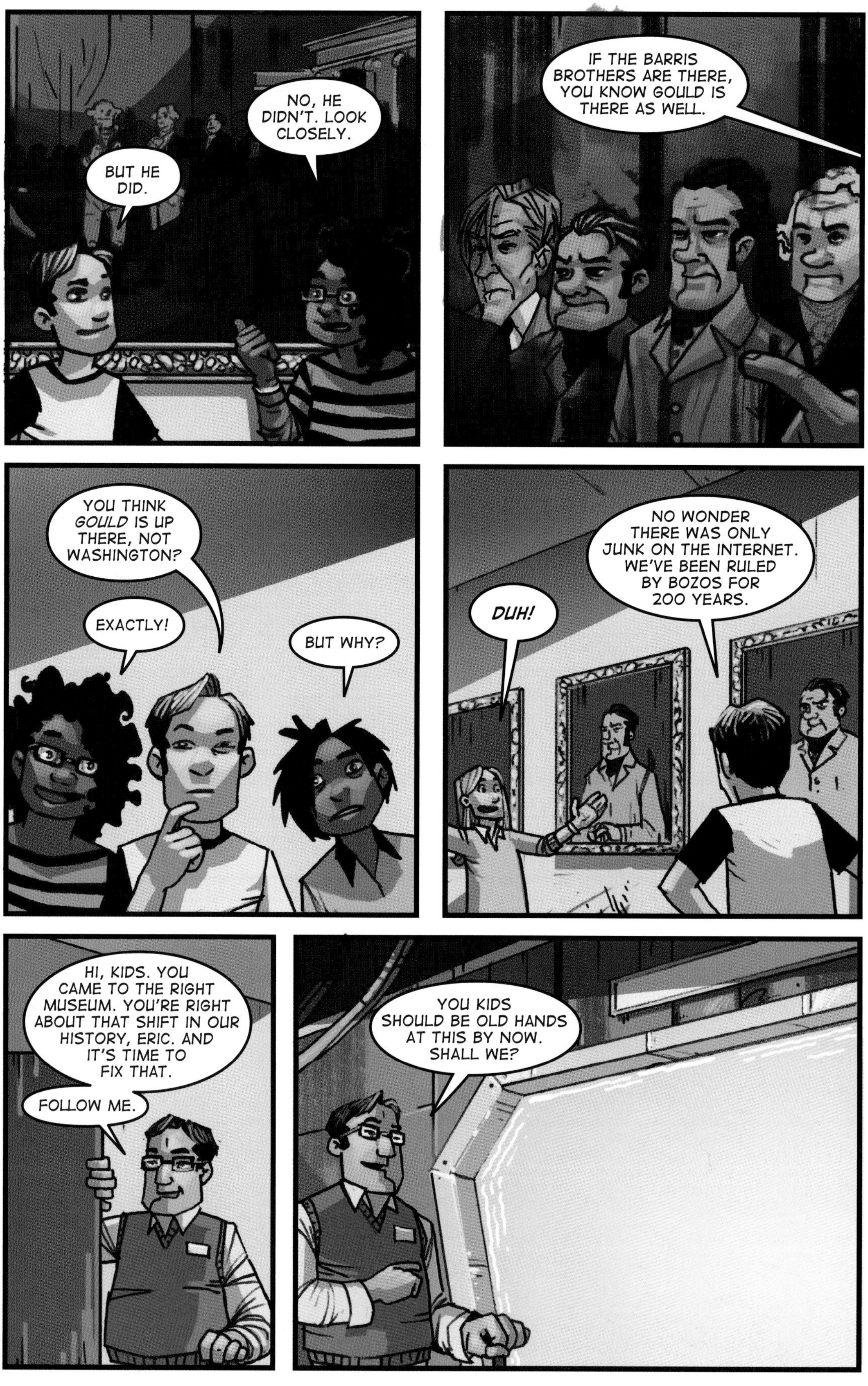
BUT HE DID.
NO, HE DIDN'T. LOOK CLOSELY.
IF THE BARRIS BROTHERS ARE THERE, YOU KNOW GOULD IS THERE AS WELL.
YOU THINK *GOULD* IS UP THERE, NOT WASHINGTON?
EXACTLY!
BUT WHY?
DUH!
NO WONDER THERE WAS ONLY JUNK ON THE INTERNET. WE'VE BEEN RULED BY BOZOS FOR 200 YEARS.
HI, KIDS. YOU CAME TO THE RIGHT MUSEUM. YOU'RE RIGHT ABOUT THAT SHIFT IN OUR HISTORY, ERIC. AND IT'S TIME TO FIX THAT.
FOLLOW ME.
YOU KIDS SHOULD BE OLD HANDS AT THIS BY NOW. SHALL WE?

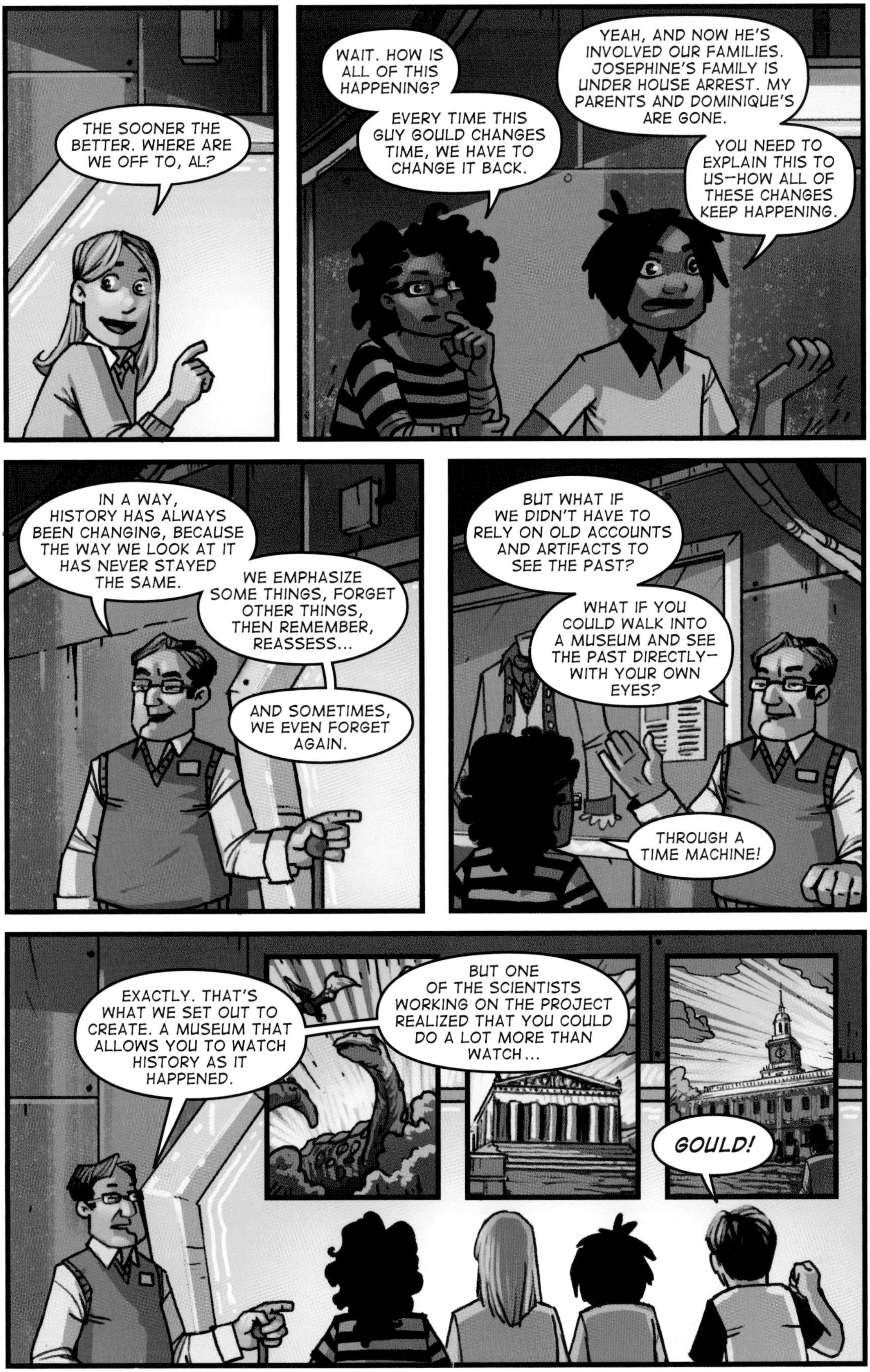
THE SOONER THE BETTER. WHERE ARE WE OFF TO, AL?
WAIT. HOW IS ALL OF THIS HAPPENING?
EVERY TIME THIS GUY GOULD CHANGES TIME, WE HAVE TO CHANGE IT BACK.
YEAH, AND NOW HE'S INVOLVED OUR FAMILIES. JOSEPHINE'S FAMILY IS UNDER HOUSE ARREST. MY PARENTS AND DOMINIQUE'S ARE GONE.
YOU NEED TO EXPLAIN THIS TO US—HOW ALL OF THESE CHANGES KEEP HAPPENING.
IN A WAY, HISTORY HAS ALWAYS BEEN CHANGING, BECAUSE THE WAY WE LOOK AT IT HAS NEVER STAYED THE SAME.
WE EMPHASIZE SOME THINGS, FORGET OTHER THINGS, THEN REMEMBER, REASSESS...
AND SOMETIMES, WE EVEN FORGET AGAIN.
BUT WHAT IF WE DIDN'T HAVE TO RELY ON OLD ACCOUNTS AND ARTIFACTS TO SEE THE PAST?
WHAT IF YOU COULD WALK INTO A MUSEUM AND SEE THE PAST DIRECTLY—WITH YOUR OWN EYES?
THROUGH A TIME MACHINE!
EXACTLY. THAT'S WHAT WE SET OUT TO CREATE. A MUSEUM THAT ALLOWS YOU TO WATCH HISTORY AS IT HAPPENED.
BUT ONE OF THE SCIENTISTS WORKING ON THE PROJECT REALIZED THAT YOU COULD DO A LOT MORE THAN WATCH...
GOULD!

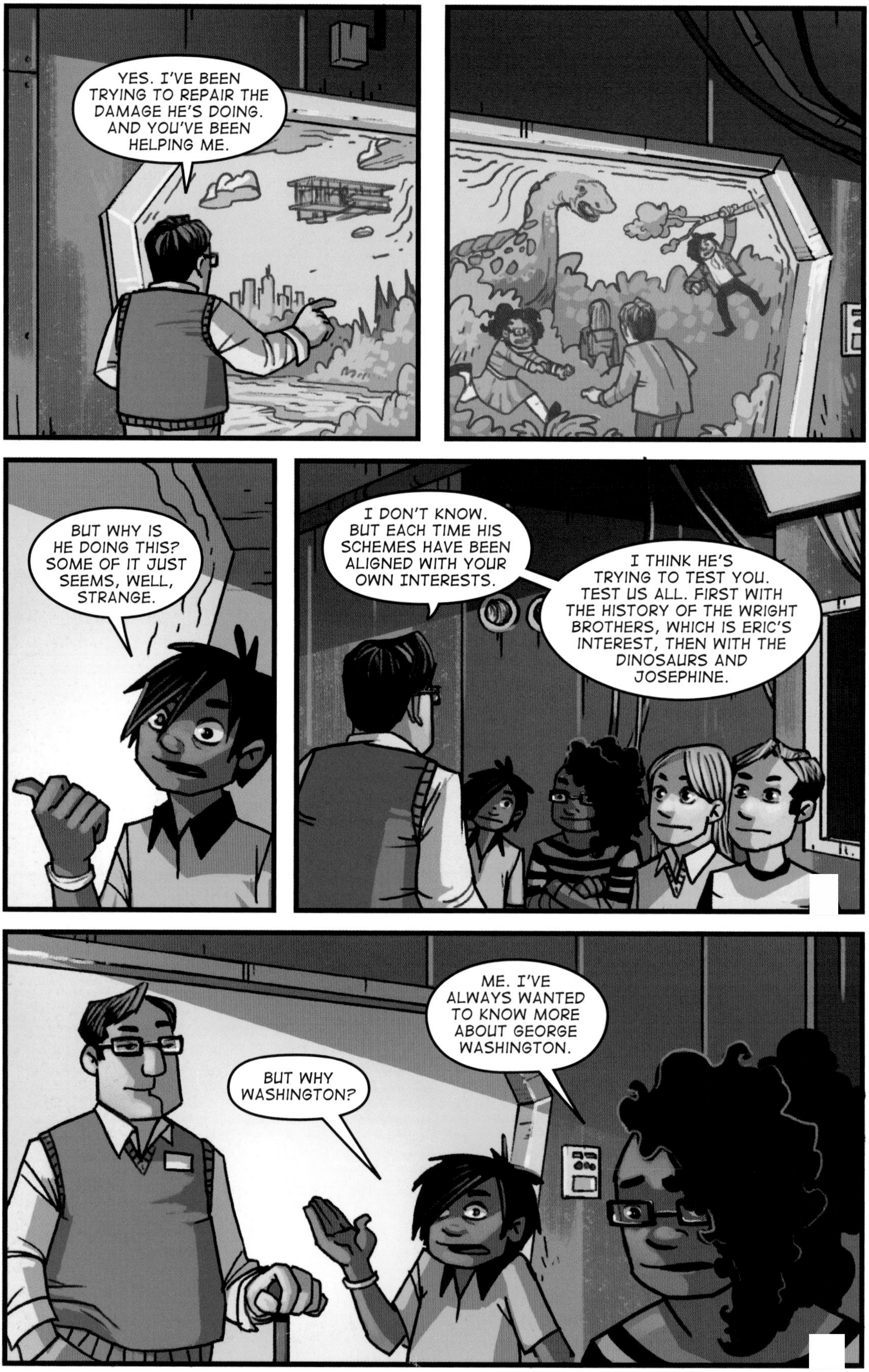
YES. I'VE BEEN TRYING TO REPAIR THE DAMAGE HE'S DOING. AND YOU'VE BEEN HELPING ME.
BUT WHY IS HE DOING THIS? SOME OF IT JUST SEEMS, WELL, STRANGE.
I DON'T KNOW. BUT EACH TIME HIS SCHEMES HAVE BEEN ALIGNED WITH YOUR OWN INTERESTS.
I THINK HE'S TRYING TO TEST YOU. TEST US ALL. FIRST WITH THE HISTORY OF THE WRIGHT BROTHERS, WHICH IS ERIC'S INTEREST, THEN WITH THE DINOSAURS AND JOSEPHINE.
BUT WHY WASHINGTON?
ME. I'VE ALWAYS WANTED TO KNOW MORE ABOUT GEORGE WASHINGTON.

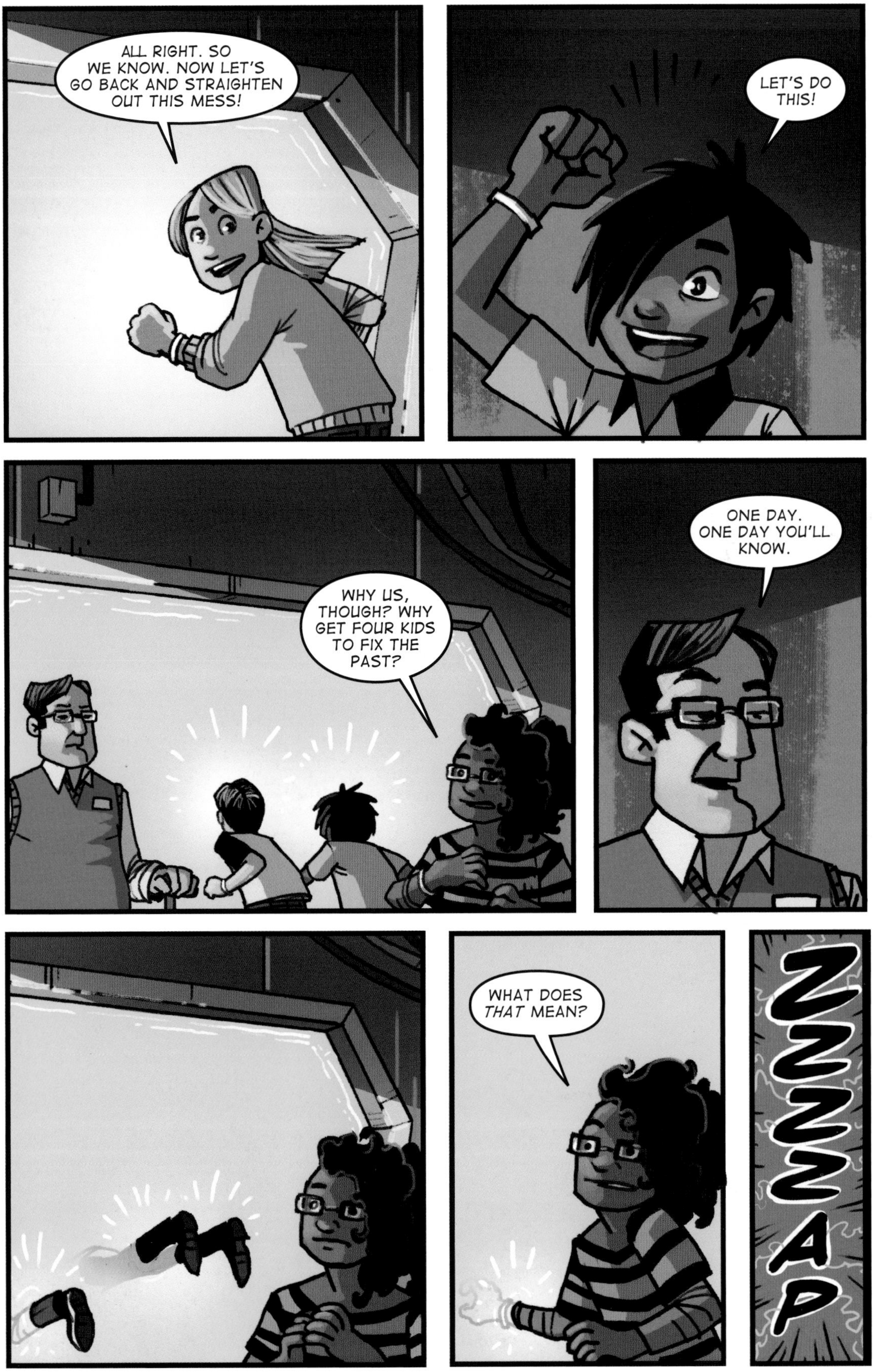
ALL RIGHT. SO WE KNOW. NOW LET'S GO BACK AND STRAIGHTEN OUT THIS MESS!
LET'S DO THIS!
WHY US, THOUGH? WHY GET FOUR KIDS TO FIX THE PAST?
ONE DAY. ONE DAY YOU'LL KNOW.
WHAT DOES *THAT* MEAN?
ZZZZAP

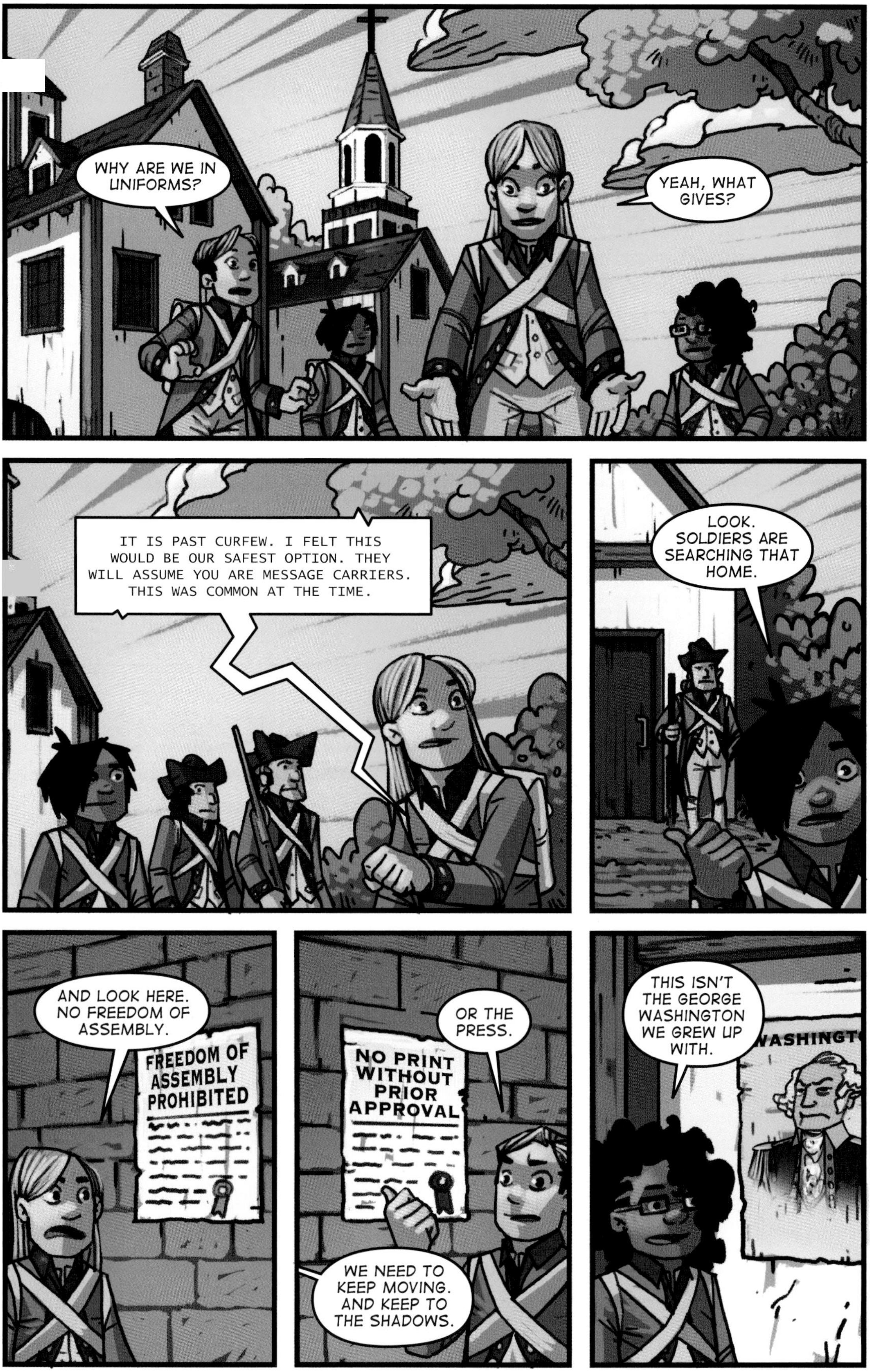
WHY ARE WE IN UNIFORMS?
YEAH, WHAT GIVES?
IT IS PAST CURFEW. I FELT THIS WOULD BE OUR SAFEST OPTION. THEY WILL ASSUME YOU ARE MESSAGE CARRIERS. THIS WAS COMMON AT THE TIME.
LOOK. SOLDIERS ARE SEARCHING THAT HOME.
AND LOOK HERE. NO FREEDOM OF ASSEMBLY.
FREEDOM OF ASSEMBLY PROHIBITED
OR THE PRESS.
NO PRINT WITHOUT PRIOR APPROVAL
WE NEED TO KEEP MOVING. AND KEEP TO THE SHADOWS.
THIS ISN'T THE GEORGE WASHINGTON WE GREW UP WITH.
WASHINGT

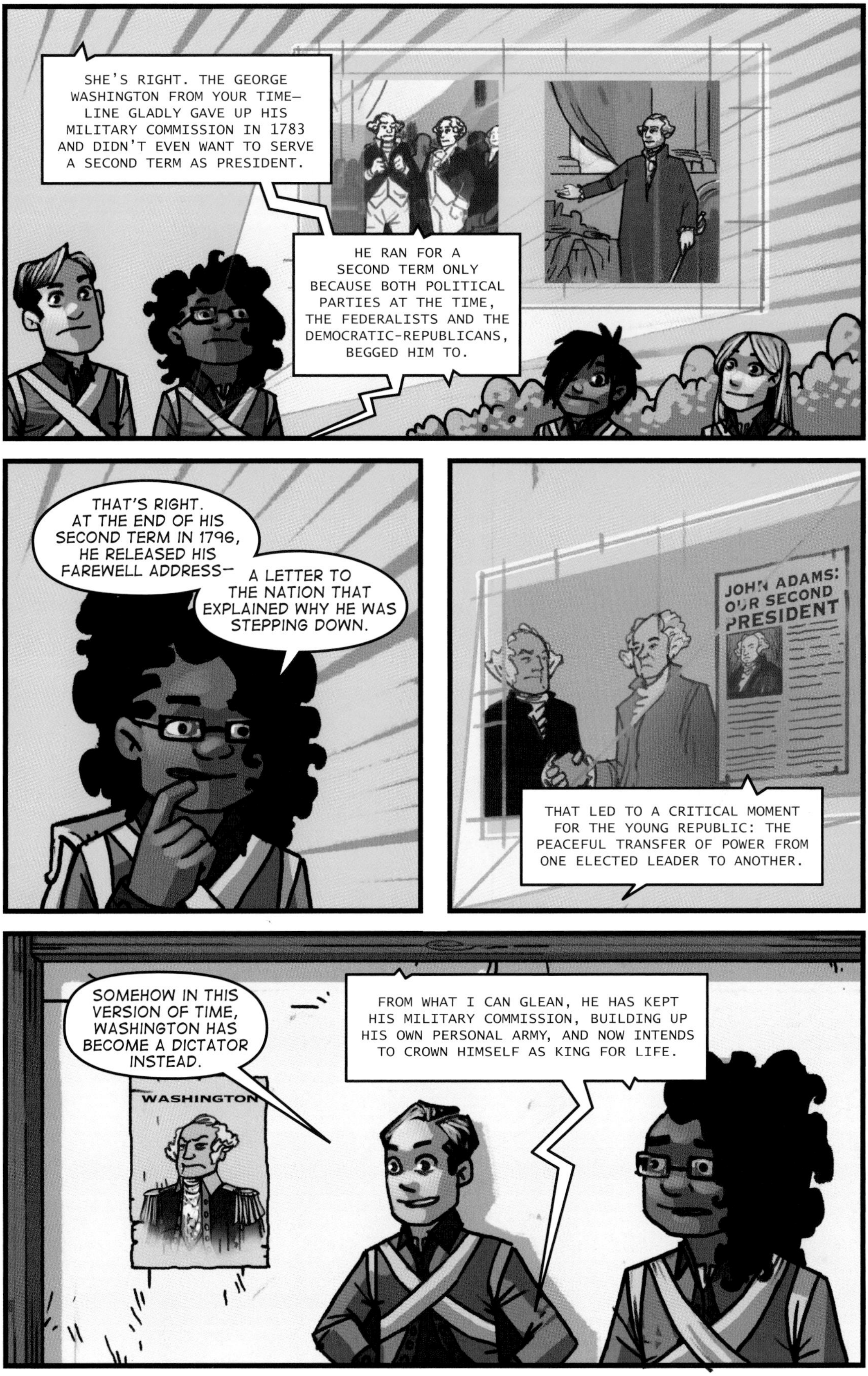
SHE'S RIGHT. THE GEORGE WASHINGTON FROM YOUR TIME-LINE GLADLY GAVE UP HIS MILITARY COMMISSION IN 1783 AND DIDN'T EVEN WANT TO SERVE A SECOND TERM AS PRESIDENT.
HE RAN FOR A SECOND TERM ONLY BECAUSE BOTH POLITICAL PARTIES AT THE TIME, THE FEDERALISTS AND THE DEMOCRATIC-REPUBLICANS, BEGGED HIM TO.
THAT'S RIGHT. AT THE END OF HIS SECOND TERM IN 1796, HE RELEASED HIS FAREWELL ADDRESS—
A LETTER TO THE NATION THAT EXPLAINED WHY HE WAS STEPPING DOWN.
JOHN ADAMS: OUR SECOND PRESIDENT
THAT LED TO A CRITICAL MOMENT FOR THE YOUNG REPUBLIC: THE PEACEFUL TRANSFER OF POWER FROM ONE ELECTED LEADER TO ANOTHER.
SOMEHOW IN THIS VERSION OF TIME, WASHINGTON HAS BECOME A DICTATOR INSTEAD.
FROM WHAT I CAN GLEAN, HE HAS KEPT HIS MILITARY COMMISSION, BUILDING UP HIS OWN PERSONAL ARMY, AND NOW INTENDS TO CROWN HIMSELF AS KING FOR LIFE.
WASHINGTON

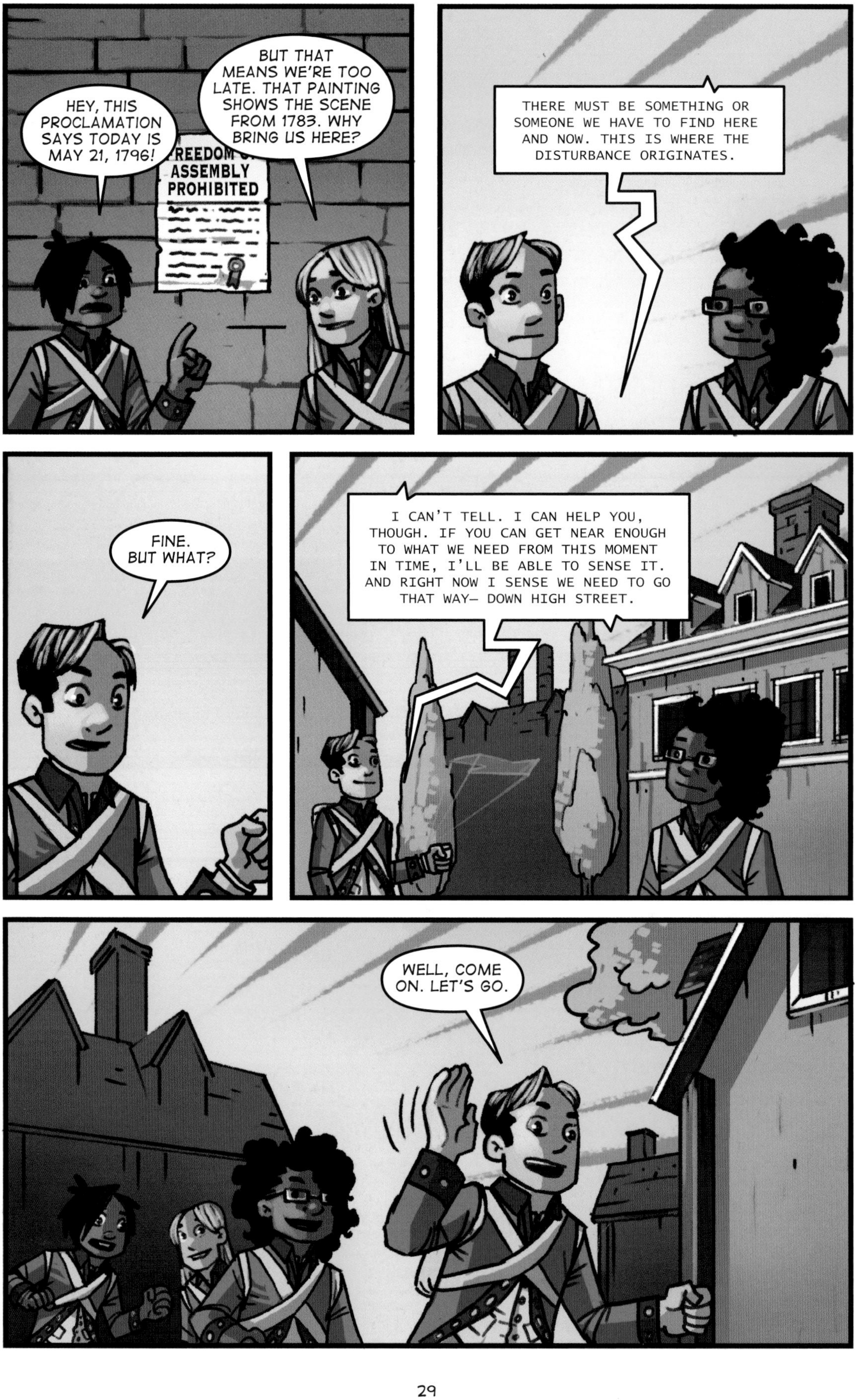
HEY, THIS PROCLAMATION SAYS TODAY IS MAY 21, 1796!
FREEDOM OF ASSEMBLY PROHIBITED
BUT THAT MEANS WE'RE TOO LATE. THAT PAINTING SHOWS THE SCENE FROM 1783. WHY BRING US HERE?
THERE MUST BE SOMETHING OR SOMEONE WE HAVE TO FIND HERE AND NOW. THIS IS WHERE THE DISTURBANCE ORIGINATES.
FINE. BUT WHAT?
I CAN'T TELL. I CAN HELP YOU, THOUGH. IF YOU CAN GET NEAR ENOUGH TO WHAT WE NEED FROM THIS MOMENT IN TIME, I'LL BE ABLE TO SENSE IT. AND RIGHT NOW I SENSE WE NEED TO GO THAT WAY— DOWN HIGH STREET.
WELL, COME ON. LET'S GO.

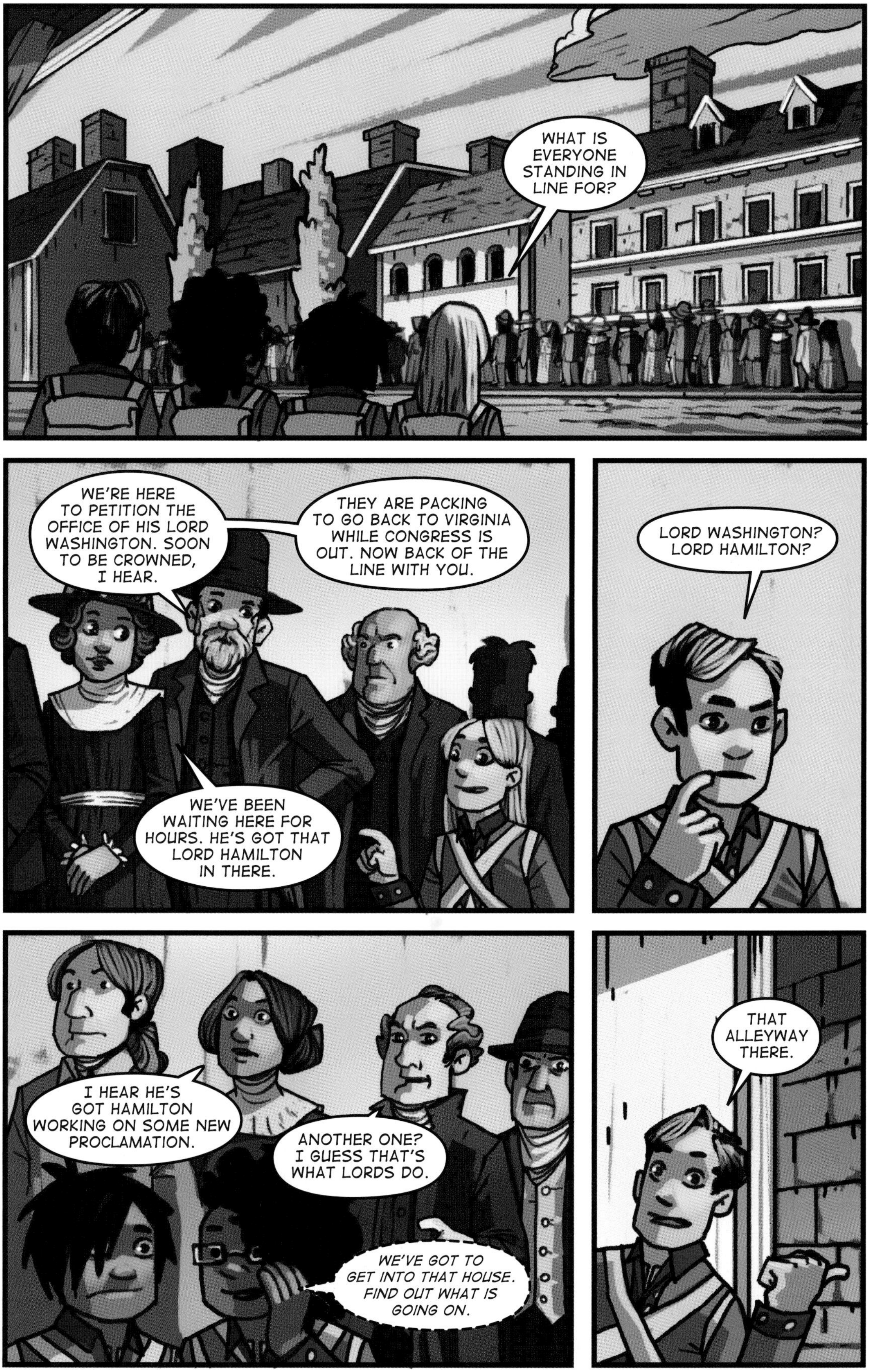
WHAT IS EVERYONE STANDING IN LINE FOR?
WE'RE HERE TO PETITION THE OFFICE OF HIS LORD WASHINGTON. SOON TO BE CROWNED, I HEAR.
THEY ARE PACKING TO GO BACK TO VIRGINIA WHILE CONGRESS IS OUT. NOW BACK OF THE LINE WITH YOU.
WE'VE BEEN WAITING HERE FOR HOURS. HE'S GOT THAT LORD HAMILTON IN THERE.
LORD WASHINGTON? LORD HAMILTON?
I HEAR HE'S GOT HAMILTON WORKING ON SOME NEW PROCLAMATION.
ANOTHER ONE? I GUESS THAT'S WHAT LORDS DO.
WE'VE GOT TO GET INTO THAT HOUSE. FIND OUT WHAT IS GOING ON.
THAT ALLEYWAY THERE.

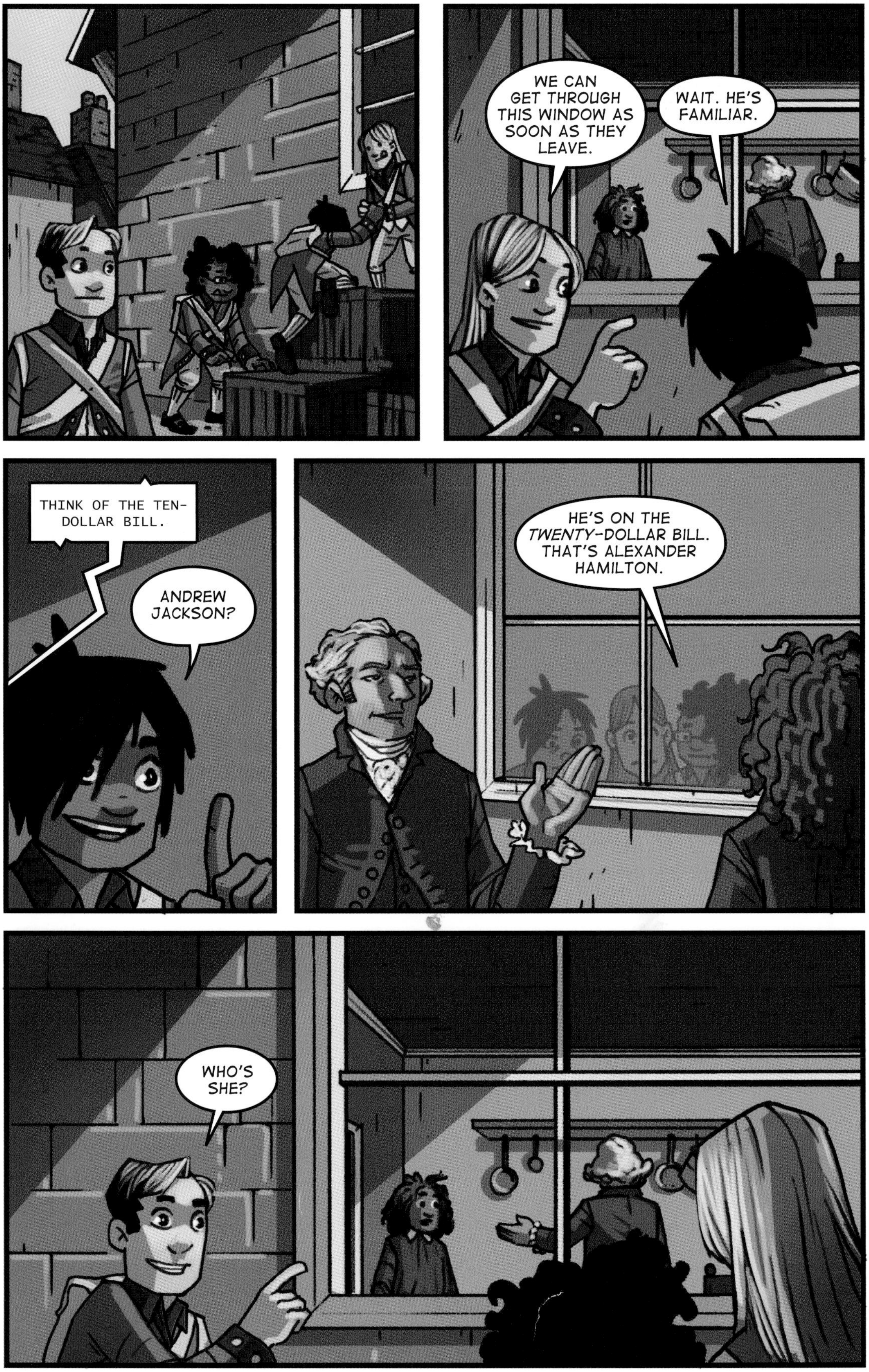
WE CAN GET THROUGH THIS WINDOW AS SOON AS THEY LEAVE.
WAIT. HE'S FAMILIAR.
THINK OF THE TEN-DOLLAR BILL.
ANDREW JACKSON?
HE'S ON THE *TWENTY*-DOLLAR BILL. THAT'S ALEXANDER HAMILTON.
WHO'S SHE?

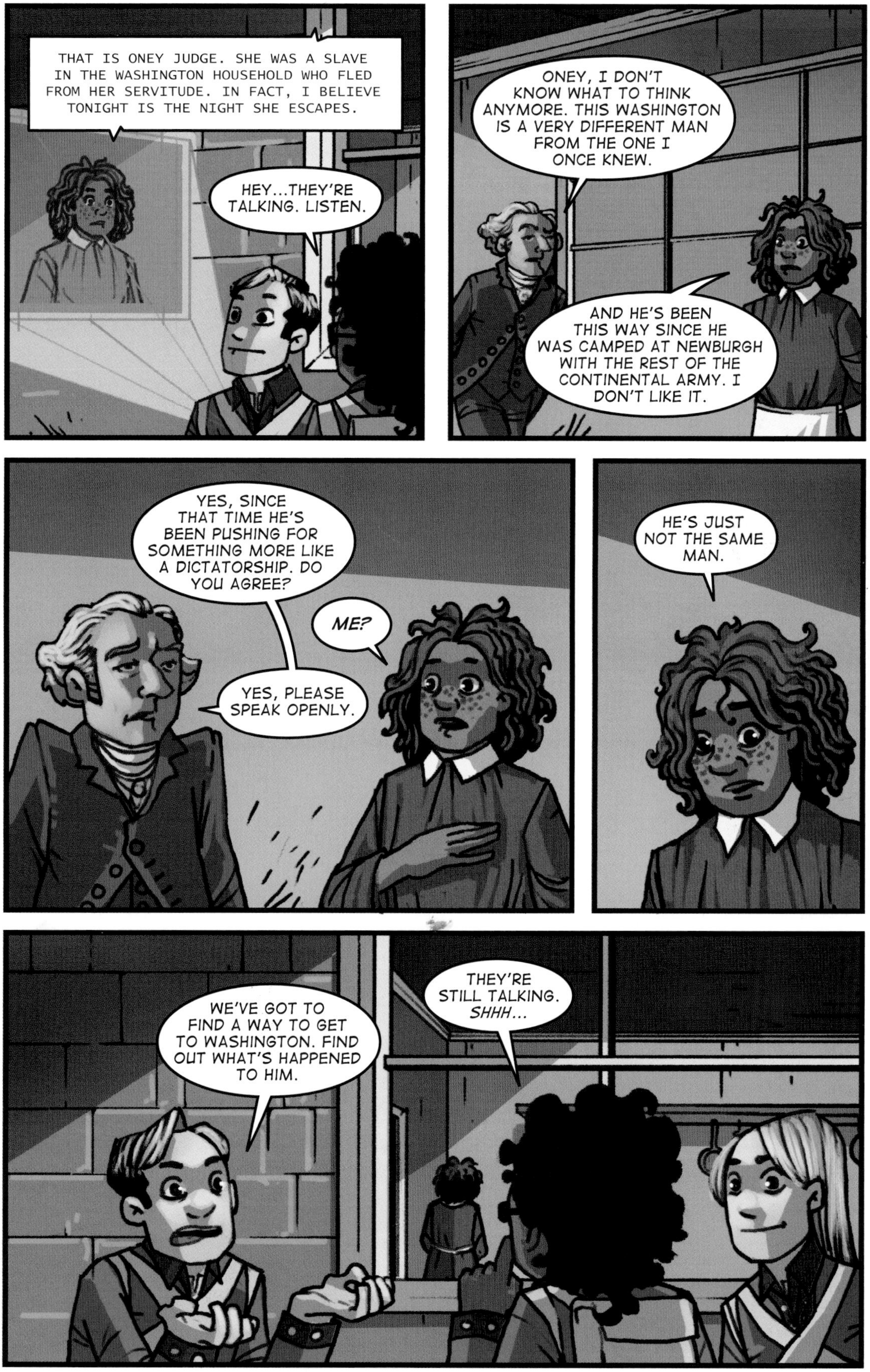
THAT IS ONEY JUDGE. SHE WAS A SLAVE IN THE WASHINGTON HOUSEHOLD WHO FLED FROM HER SERVITUDE. IN FACT, I BELIEVE TONIGHT IS THE NIGHT SHE ESCAPES.
HEY...THEY'RE TALKING. LISTEN.
ONEY, I DON'T KNOW WHAT TO THINK ANYMORE. THIS WASHINGTON IS A VERY DIFFERENT MAN FROM THE ONE I ONCE KNEW.
AND HE'S BEEN THIS WAY SINCE HE WAS CAMPED AT NEWBURGH WITH THE REST OF THE CONTINENTAL ARMY. I DON'T LIKE IT.
YES, SINCE THAT TIME HE'S BEEN PUSHING FOR SOMETHING MORE LIKE A DICTATORSHIP. DO YOU AGREE?
ME?
YES, PLEASE SPEAK OPENLY.
HE'S JUST NOT THE SAME MAN.
WE'VE GOT TO FIND A WAY TO GET TO WASHINGTON. FIND OUT WHAT'S HAPPENED TO HIM.
THEY'RE STILL TALKING. *SHHH...*

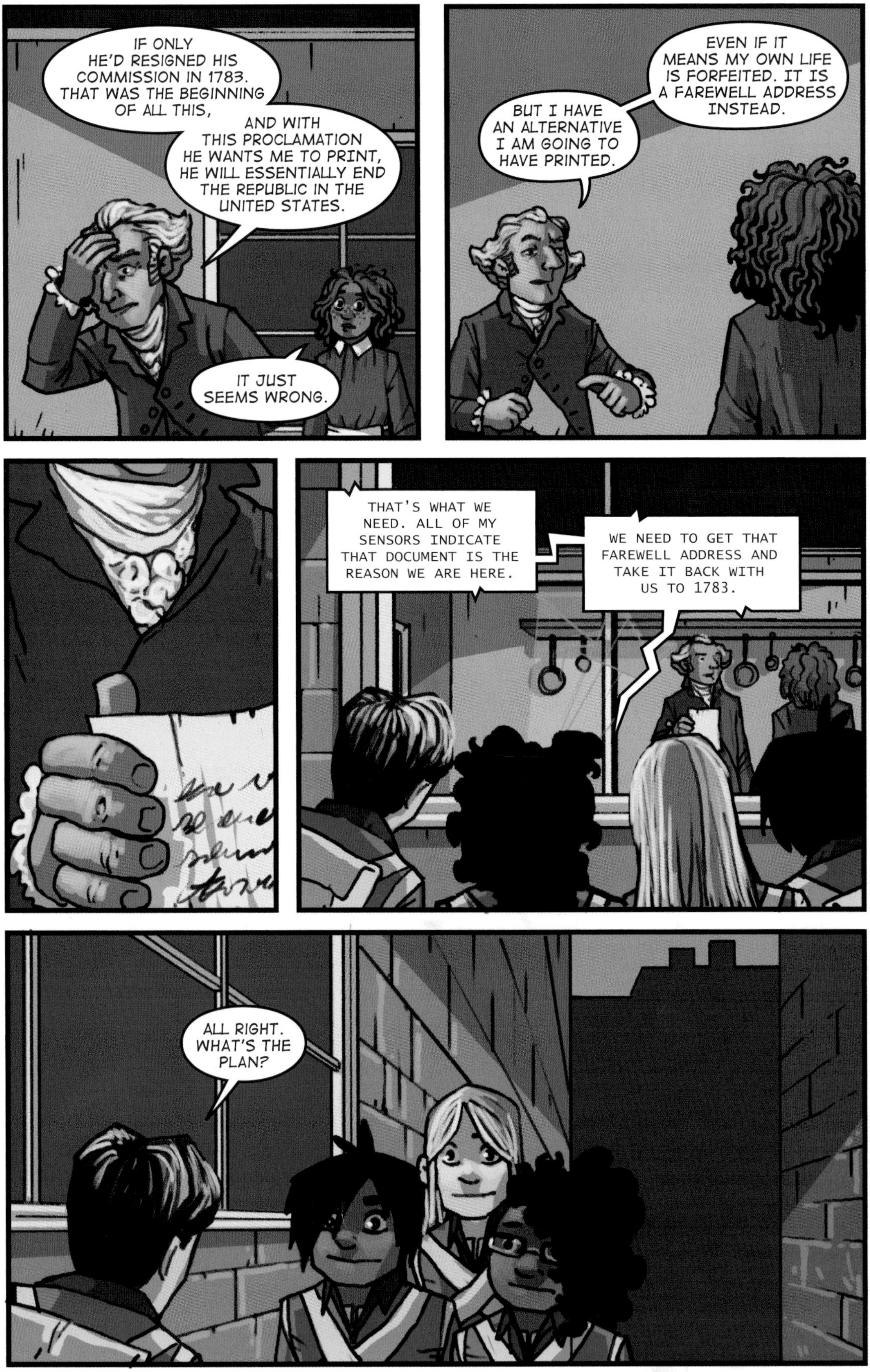
IF ONLY HE'D RESIGNED HIS COMMISSION IN 1783. THAT WAS THE BEGINNING OF ALL THIS,
AND WITH THIS PROCLAMATION HE WANTS ME TO PRINT, HE WILL ESSENTIALLY END THE REPUBLIC IN THE UNITED STATES.
IT JUST SEEMS WRONG.
BUT I HAVE AN ALTERNATIVE I AM GOING TO HAVE PRINTED.
EVEN IF IT MEANS MY OWN LIFE IS FORFEITED. IT IS A FAREWELL ADDRESS INSTEAD.
THAT'S WHAT WE NEED. ALL OF MY SENSORS INDICATE THAT DOCUMENT IS THE REASON WE ARE HERE.
WE NEED TO GET THAT FAREWELL ADDRESS AND TAKE IT BACK WITH US TO 1783.
ALL RIGHT. WHAT'S THE PLAN?

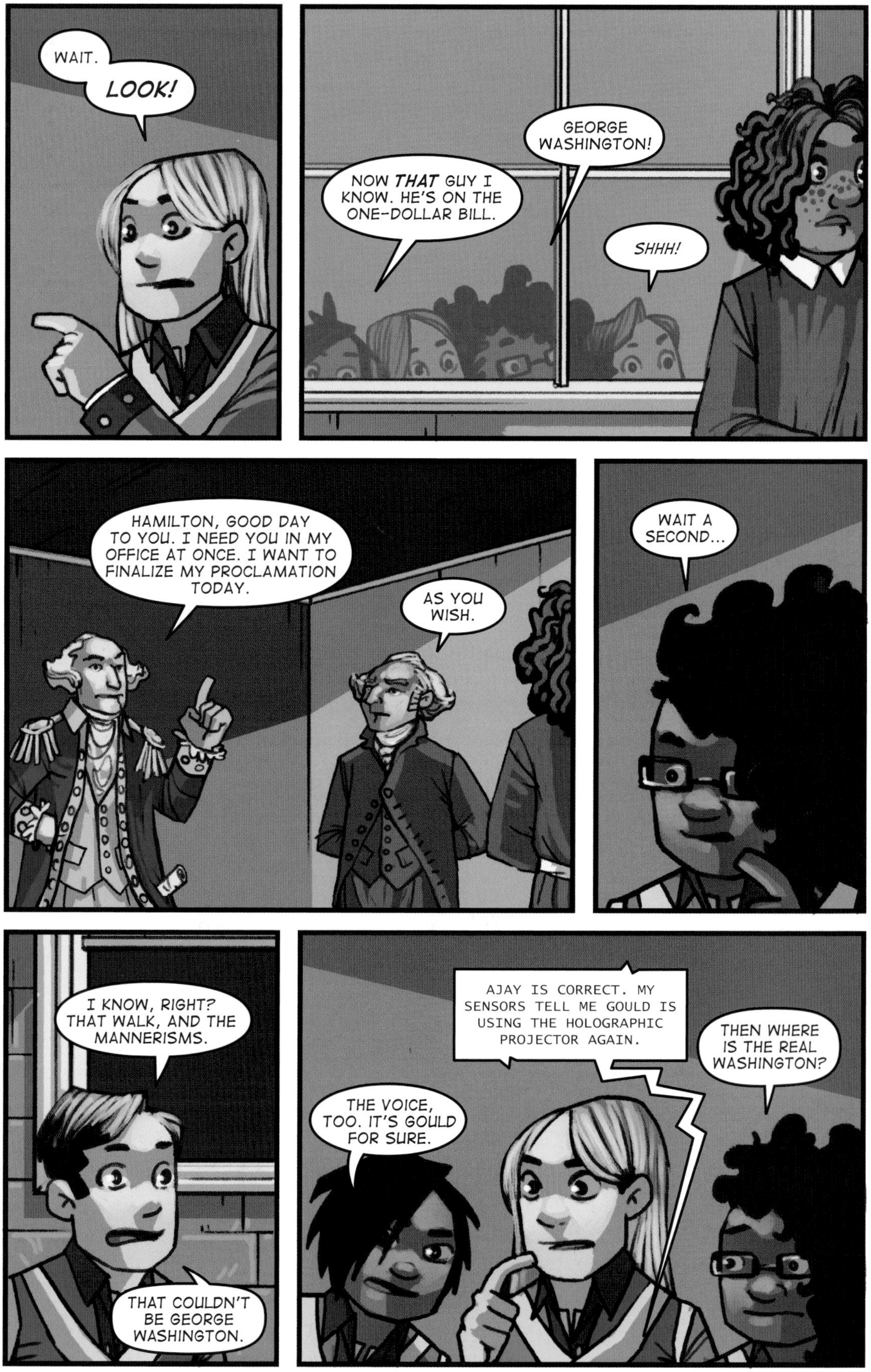
WAIT.
LOOK!
NOW *THAT* GUY I KNOW. HE'S ON THE ONE-DOLLAR BILL.
GEORGE WASHINGTON!
SHHH!
HAMILTON, GOOD DAY TO YOU. I NEED YOU IN MY OFFICE AT ONCE. I WANT TO FINALIZE MY PROCLAMATION TODAY.
AS YOU WISH.
WAIT A SECOND...
I KNOW, RIGHT? THAT WALK, AND THE MANNERISMS.
THAT COULDN'T BE GEORGE WASHINGTON.
AJAY IS CORRECT. MY SENSORS TELL ME GOULD IS USING THE HOLOGRAPHIC PROJECTOR AGAIN.
THEN WHERE IS THE REAL WASHINGTON?
THE VOICE, TOO. IT'S GOULD FOR SURE.

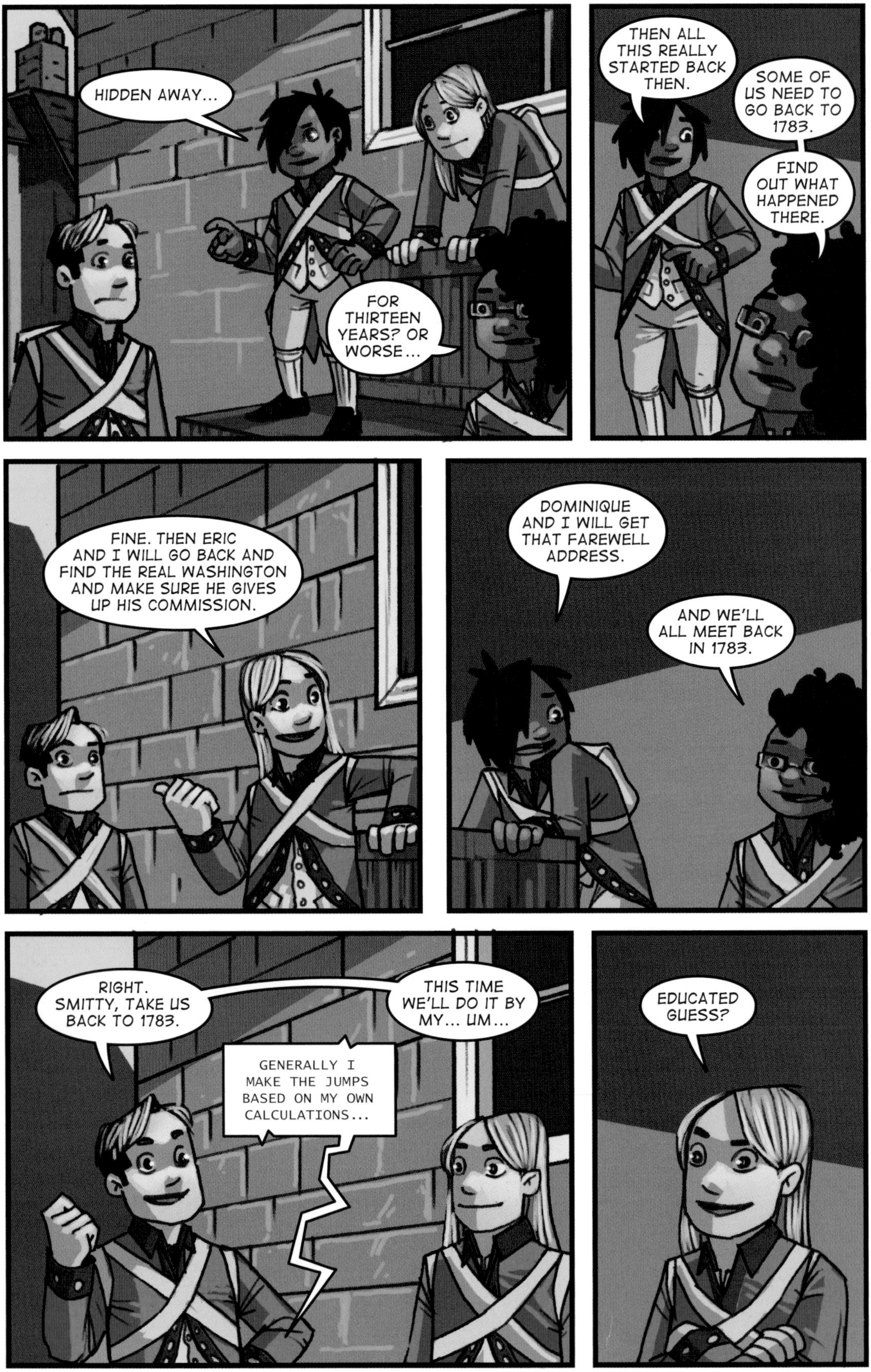
HIDDEN AWAY...
FOR THIRTEEN YEARS? OR WORSE...
THEN ALL THIS REALLY STARTED BACK THEN.
SOME OF US NEED TO GO BACK TO 1783.
FIND OUT WHAT HAPPENED THERE.
FINE. THEN ERIC AND I WILL GO BACK AND FIND THE REAL WASHINGTON AND MAKE SURE HE GIVES UP HIS COMMISSION.
DOMINIQUE AND I WILL GET THAT FAREWELL ADDRESS.
AND WE'LL ALL MEET BACK IN 1783.
RIGHT. SMITTY, TAKE US BACK TO 1783.
THIS TIME WE'LL DO IT BY MY... UM...
GENERALLY I MAKE THE JUMPS BASED ON MY OWN CALCULATIONS...
EDUCATED GUESS?

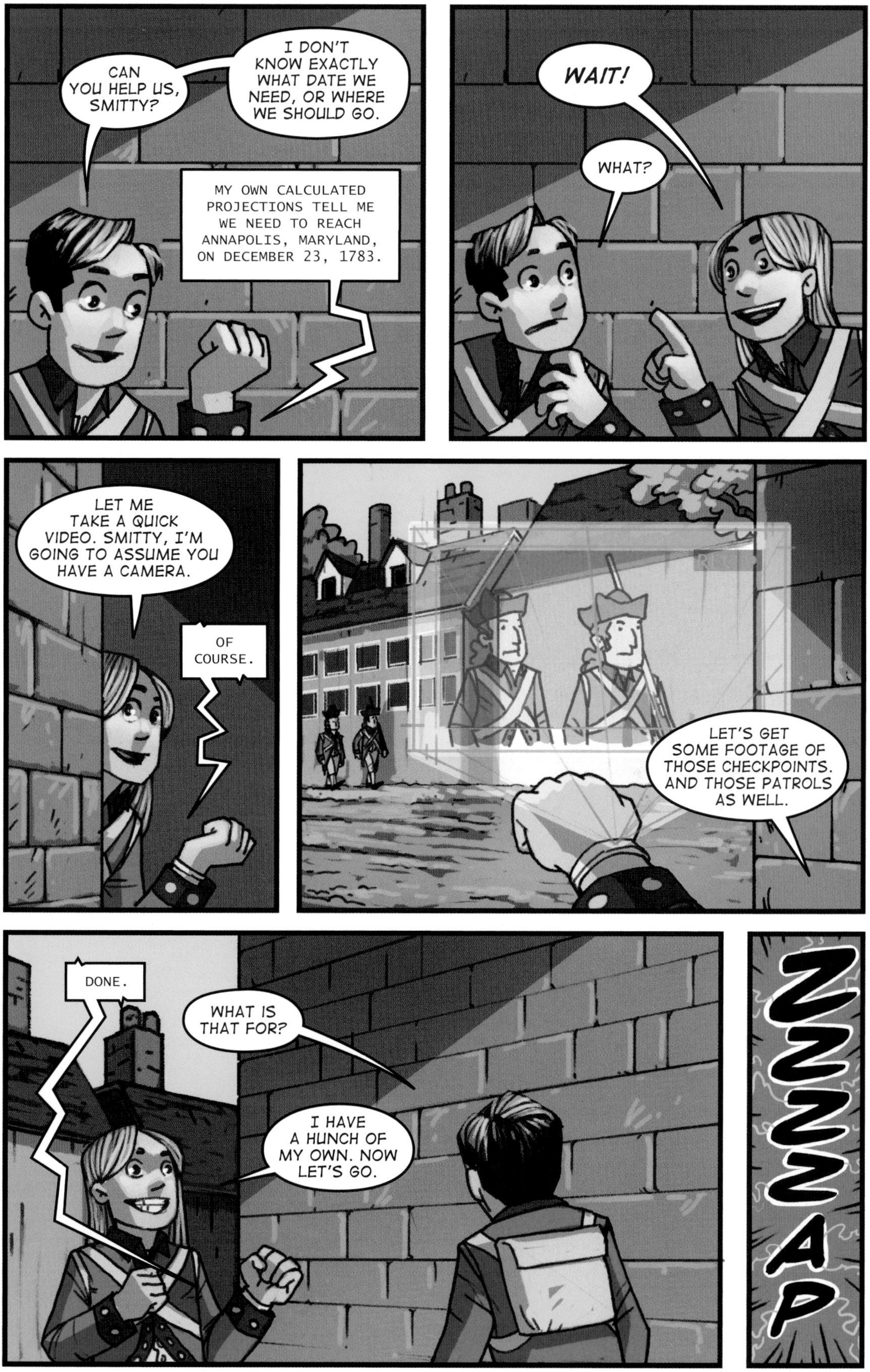
CAN YOU HELP US, SMITTY?
I DON'T KNOW EXACTLY WHAT DATE WE NEED, OR WHERE WE SHOULD GO.
MY OWN CALCULATED PROJECTIONS TELL ME WE NEED TO REACH ANNAPOLIS, MARYLAND, ON DECEMBER 23, 1783.
WAIT!
WHAT?
LET ME TAKE A QUICK VIDEO. SMITTY, I'M GOING TO ASSUME YOU HAVE A CAMERA.
OF COURSE.
LET'S GET SOME FOOTAGE OF THOSE CHECKPOINTS. AND THOSE PATROLS AS WELL.
DONE.
WHAT IS THAT FOR?
I HAVE A HUNCH OF MY OWN. NOW LET'S GO.
ZZZZAP

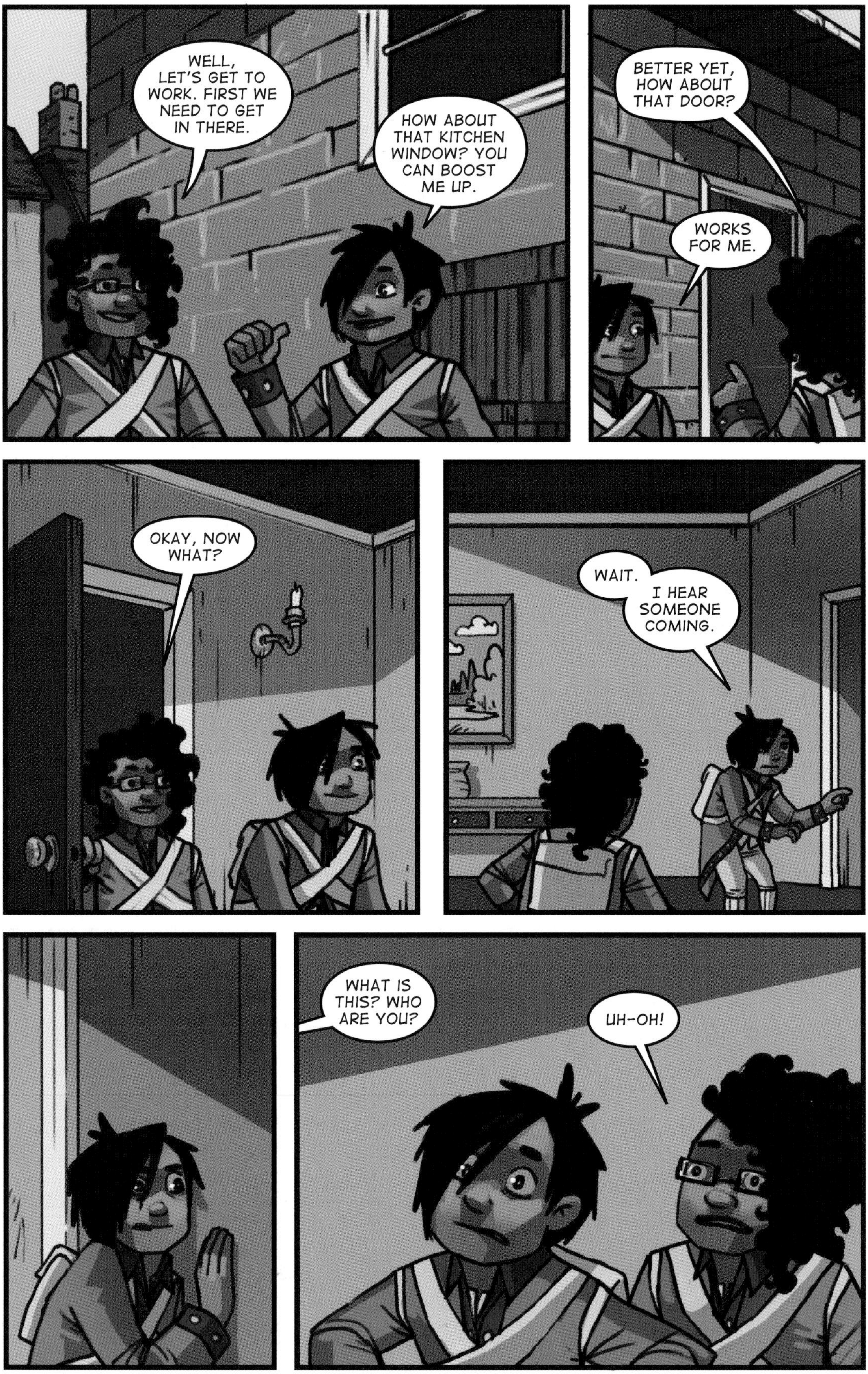
WELL, LET'S GET TO WORK. FIRST WE NEED TO GET IN THERE.
HOW ABOUT THAT KITCHEN WINDOW? YOU CAN BOOST ME UP.
BETTER YET, HOW ABOUT THAT DOOR?
WORKS FOR ME.
OKAY, NOW WHAT?
WAIT.
I HEAR SOMEONE COMING.
WHAT IS THIS? WHO ARE YOU?
UH-OH!

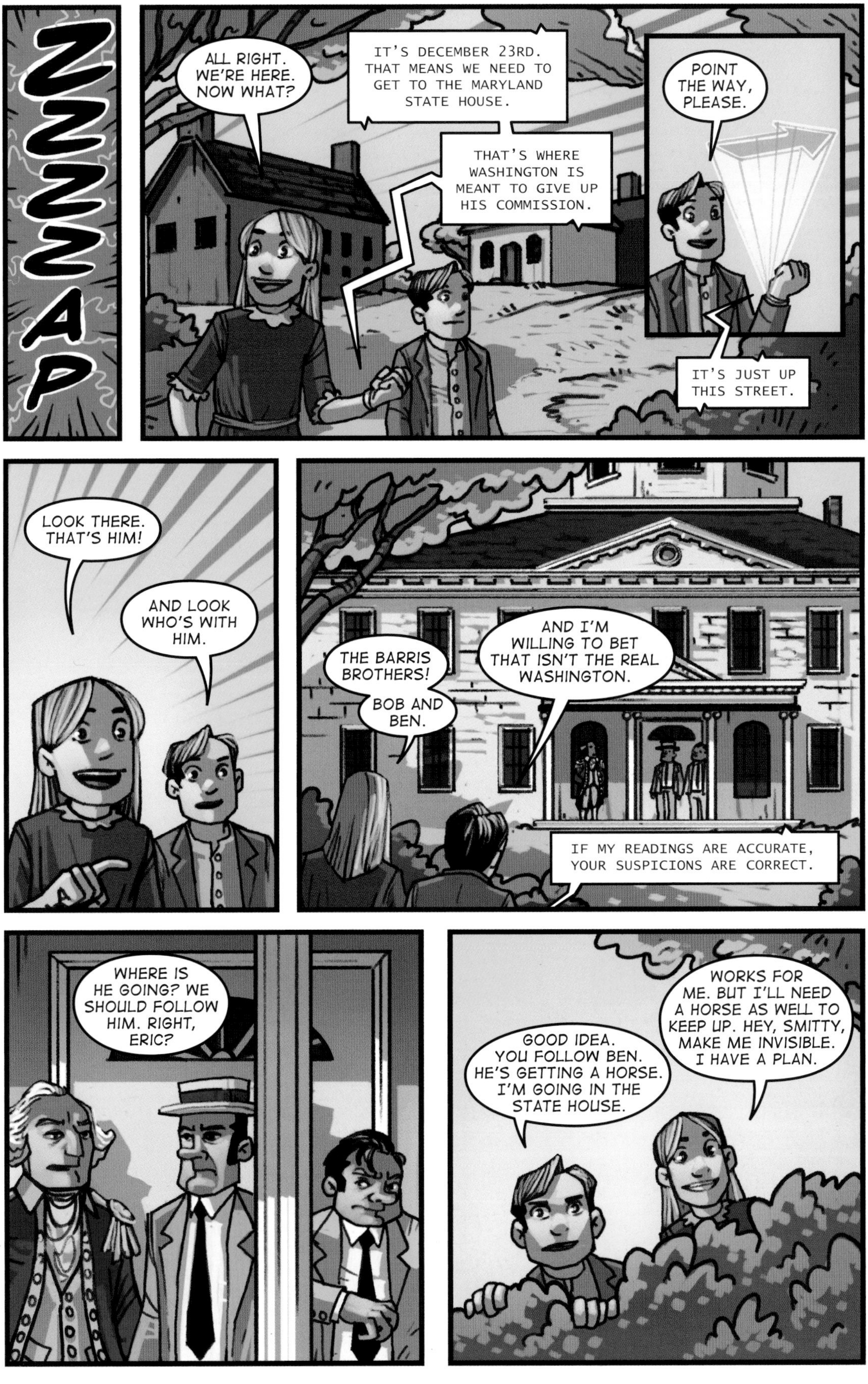
ZZZZZAP
ALL RIGHT. WE'RE HERE. NOW WHAT?
IT'S DECEMBER 23RD. THAT MEANS WE NEED TO GET TO THE MARYLAND STATE HOUSE.
THAT'S WHERE WASHINGTON IS MEANT TO GIVE UP HIS COMMISSION.
POINT THE WAY, PLEASE.
IT'S JUST UP THIS STREET.
LOOK THERE. THAT'S HIM!
AND LOOK WHO'S WITH HIM.
THE BARRIS BROTHERS!
BOB AND BEN.
AND I'M WILLING TO BET THAT ISN'T THE REAL WASHINGTON.
IF MY READINGS ARE ACCURATE, YOUR SUSPICIONS ARE CORRECT.
WHERE IS HE GOING? WE SHOULD FOLLOW HIM. RIGHT, ERIC?
GOOD IDEA. YOU FOLLOW BEN. HE'S GETTING A HORSE. I'M GOING IN THE STATE HOUSE.
WORKS FOR ME. BUT I'LL NEED A HORSE AS WELL TO KEEP UP. HEY, SMITTY, MAKE ME INVISIBLE. I HAVE A PLAN.

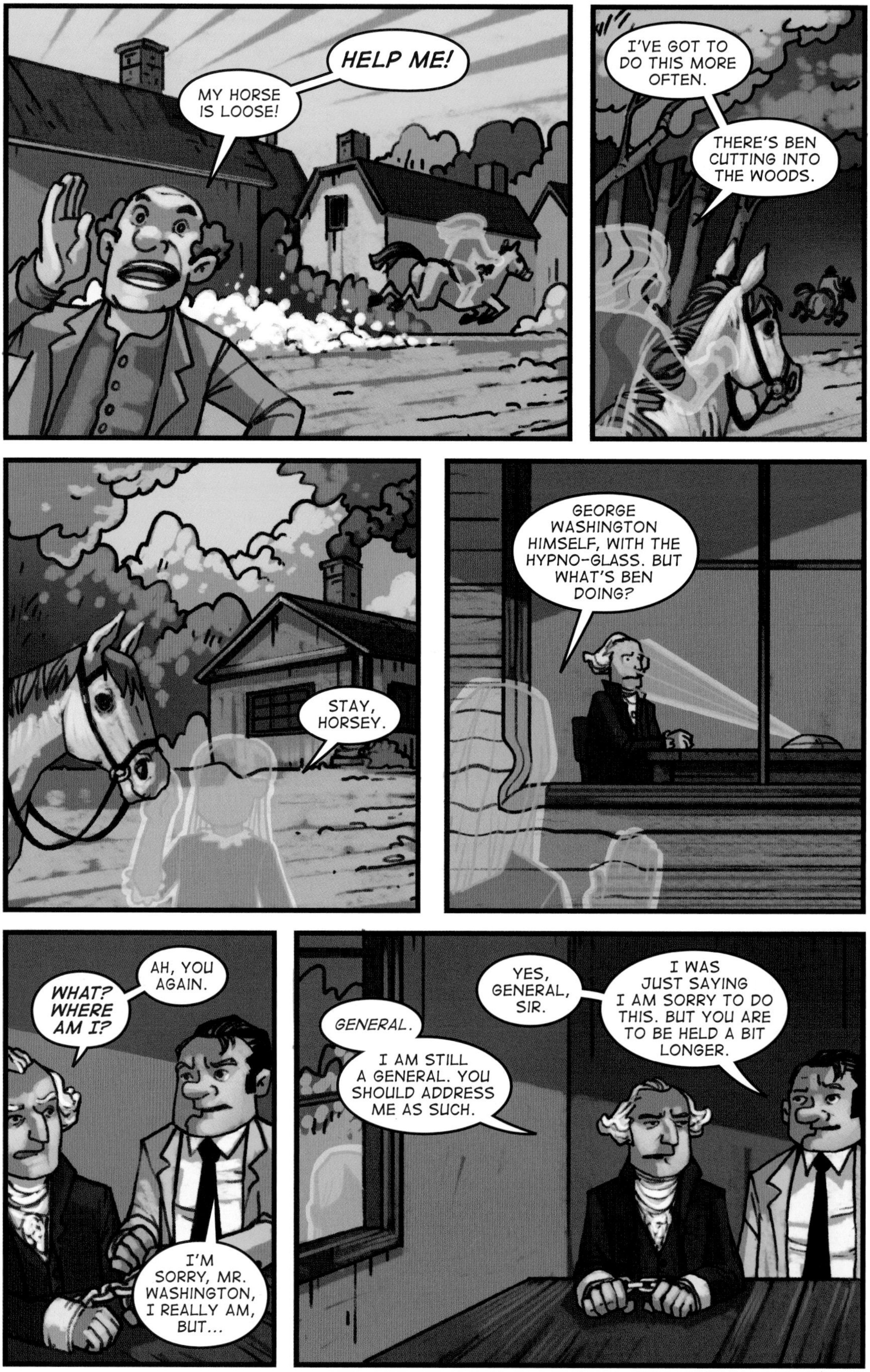
HELP ME!
MY HORSE IS LOOSE!
I'VE GOT TO DO THIS MORE OFTEN.
THERE'S BEN CUTTING INTO THE WOODS.
STAY, HORSEY.
GEORGE WASHINGTON HIMSELF, WITH THE HYPNO-GLASS. BUT WHAT'S BEN DOING?
WHAT? WHERE AM I?
AH, YOU AGAIN.
I'M SORRY, MR. WASHINGTON, I REALLY AM, BUT...
GENERAL.
I AM STILL A GENERAL. YOU SHOULD ADDRESS ME AS SUCH.
YES, GENERAL, SIR.
I WAS JUST SAYING I AM SORRY TO DO THIS. BUT YOU ARE TO BE HELD A BIT LONGER.

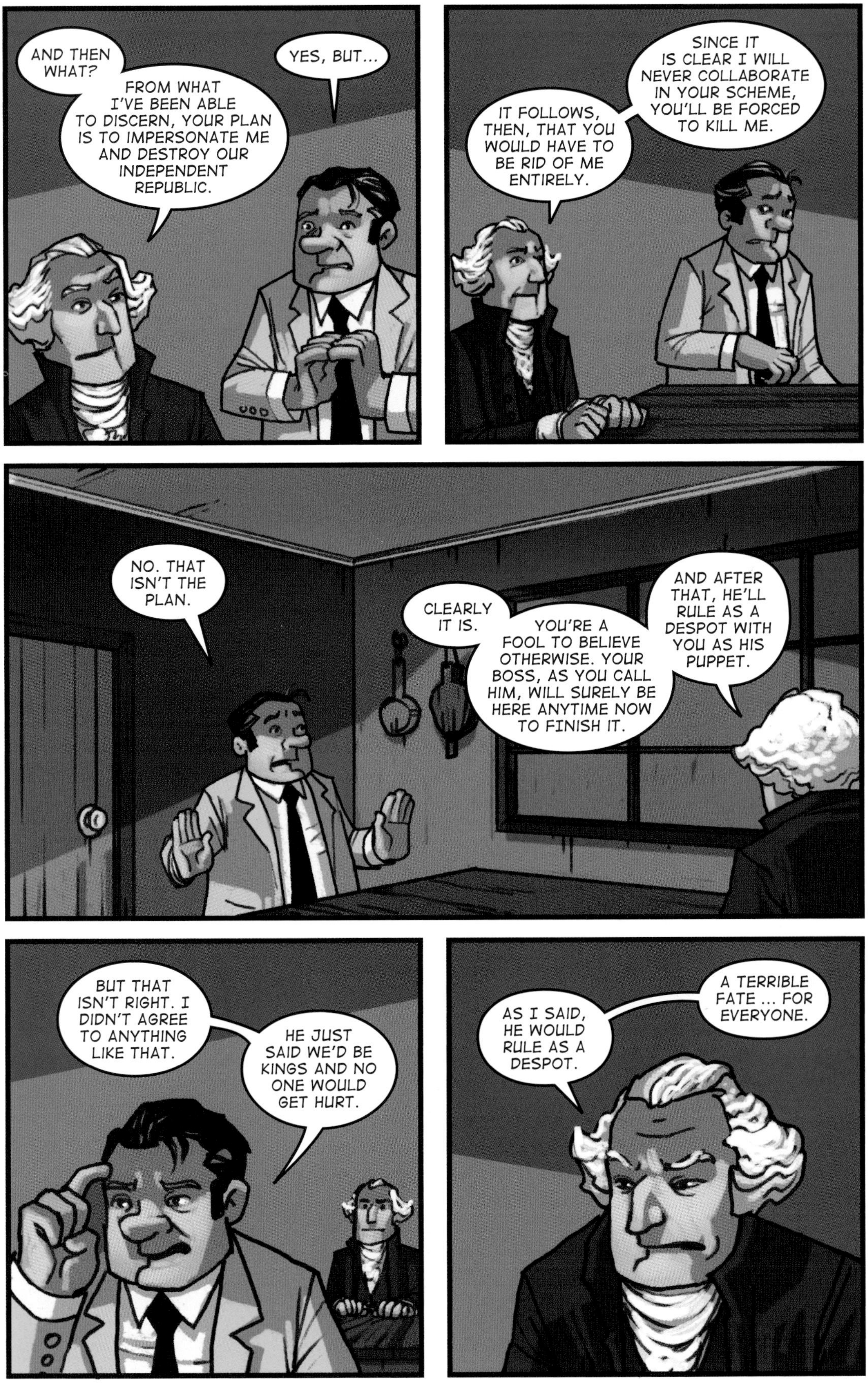
AND THEN WHAT?
FROM WHAT I'VE BEEN ABLE TO DISCERN, YOUR PLAN IS TO IMPERSONATE ME AND DESTROY OUR INDEPENDENT REPUBLIC.
YES, BUT...
IT FOLLOWS, THEN, THAT YOU WOULD HAVE TO BE RID OF ME ENTIRELY.
SINCE IT IS CLEAR I WILL NEVER COLLABORATE IN YOUR SCHEME, YOU'LL BE FORCED TO KILL ME.
NO. THAT ISN'T THE PLAN.
CLEARLY IT IS.
YOU'RE A FOOL TO BELIEVE OTHERWISE. YOUR BOSS, AS YOU CALL HIM, WILL SURELY BE HERE ANYTIME NOW TO FINISH IT.
AND AFTER THAT, HE'LL RULE AS A DESPOT WITH YOU AS HIS PUPPET.
BUT THAT ISN'T RIGHT. I DIDN'T AGREE TO ANYTHING LIKE THAT.
HE JUST SAID WE'D BE KINGS AND NO ONE WOULD GET HURT.
AS I SAID, HE WOULD RULE AS A DESPOT.
A TERRIBLE FATE ... FOR EVERYONE.

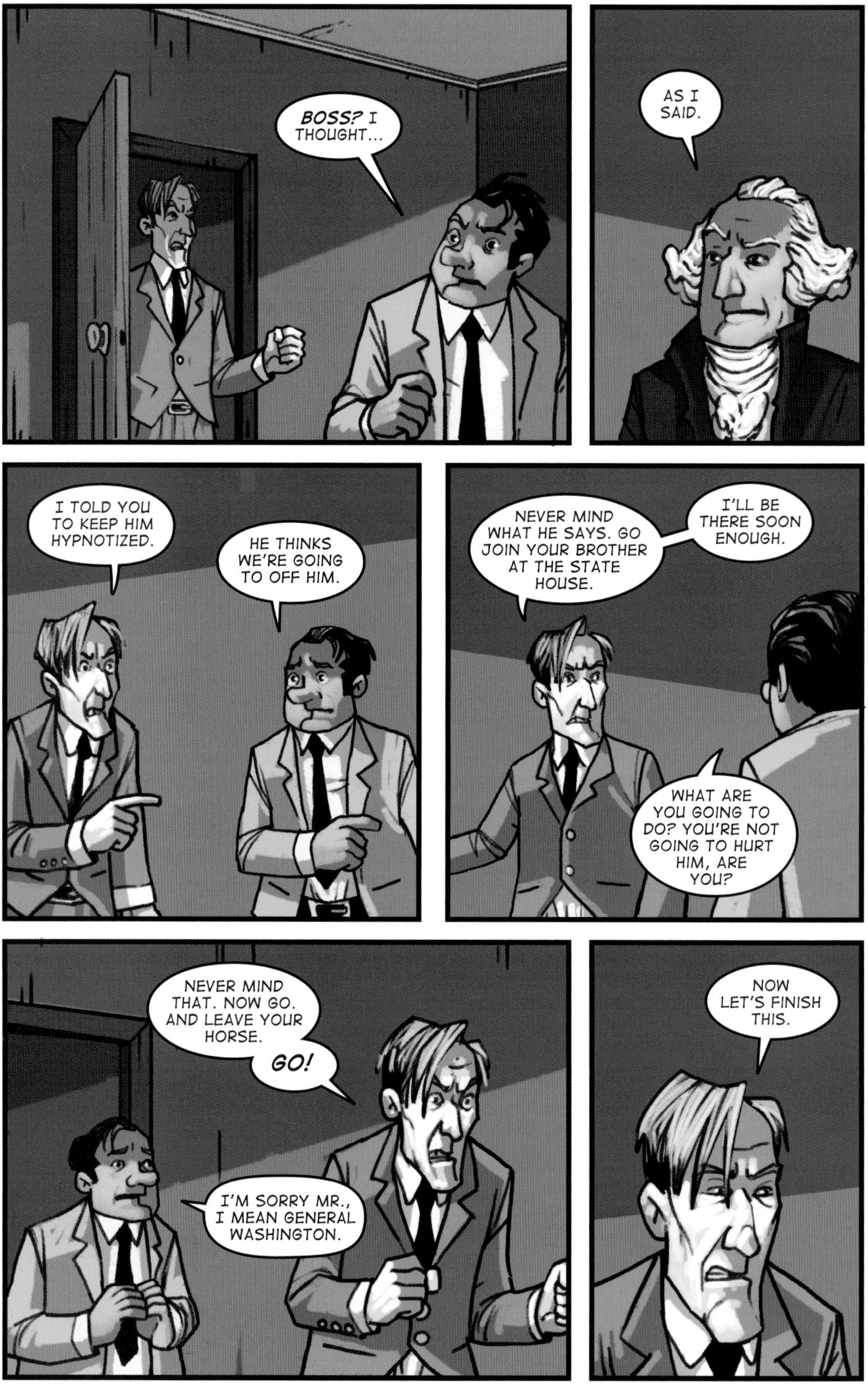
BOSS? I THOUGHT...
AS I SAID.
I TOLD YOU TO KEEP HIM HYPNOTIZED.
HE THINKS WE'RE GOING TO OFF HIM.
NEVER MIND WHAT HE SAYS. GO JOIN YOUR BROTHER AT THE STATE HOUSE.
I'LL BE THERE SOON ENOUGH.
WHAT ARE YOU GOING TO DO? YOU'RE NOT GOING TO HURT HIM, ARE YOU?
NEVER MIND THAT. NOW GO. AND LEAVE YOUR HORSE.
GO!
I'M SORRY MR., I MEAN GENERAL WASHINGTON.
NOW LET'S FINISH THIS.

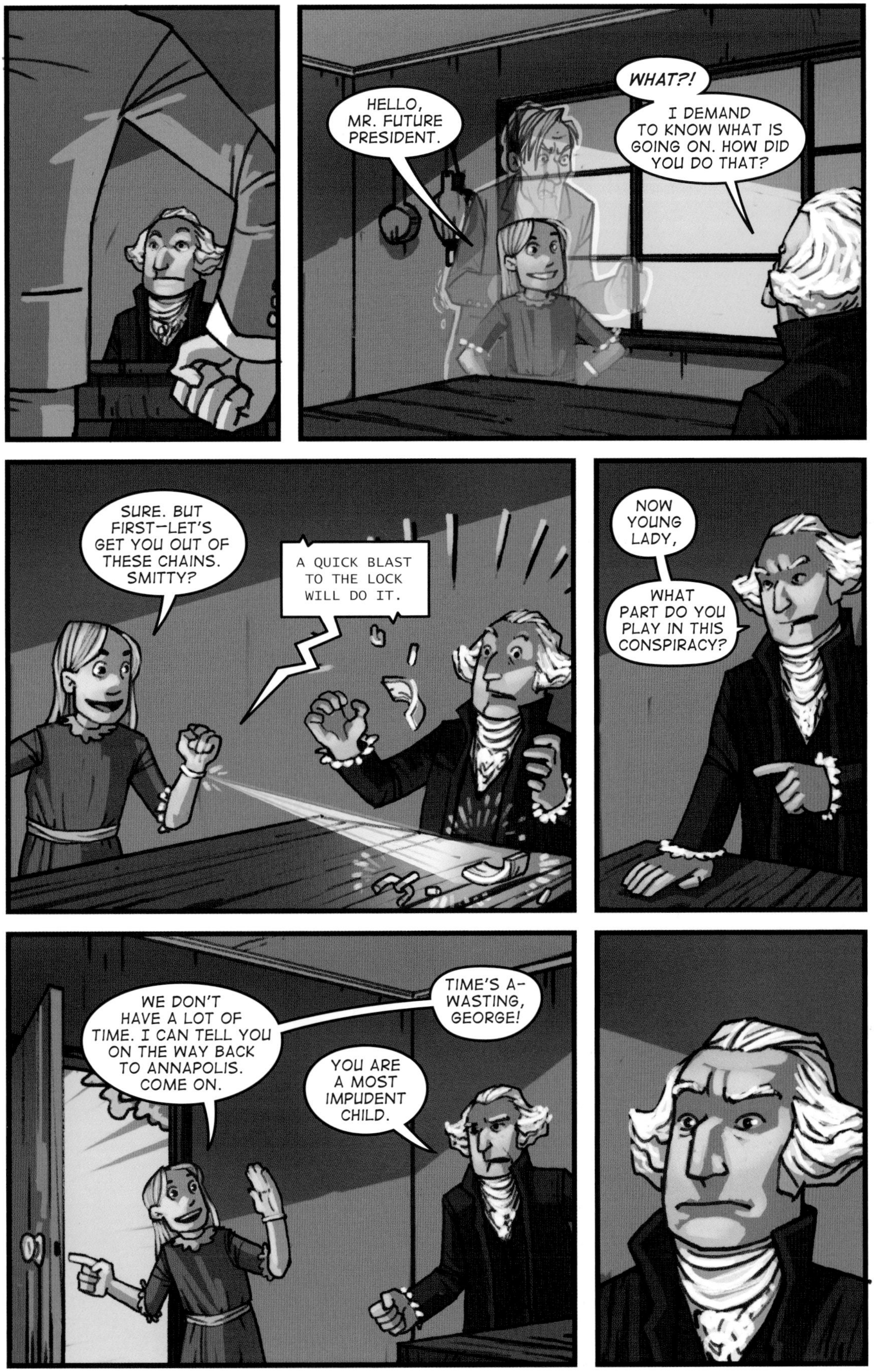
HELLO, MR. FUTURE PRESIDENT.
WHAT?!
I DEMAND TO KNOW WHAT IS GOING ON. HOW DID YOU DO THAT?
SURE. BUT FIRST—LET'S GET YOU OUT OF THESE CHAINS. SMITTY?
A QUICK BLAST TO THE LOCK WILL DO IT.
NOW YOUNG LADY,
WHAT PART DO YOU PLAY IN THIS CONSPIRACY?
WE DON'T HAVE A LOT OF TIME. I CAN TELL YOU ON THE WAY BACK TO ANNAPOLIS. COME ON.
TIME'S A-WASTING, GEORGE!
YOU ARE A MOST IMPUDENT CHILD.

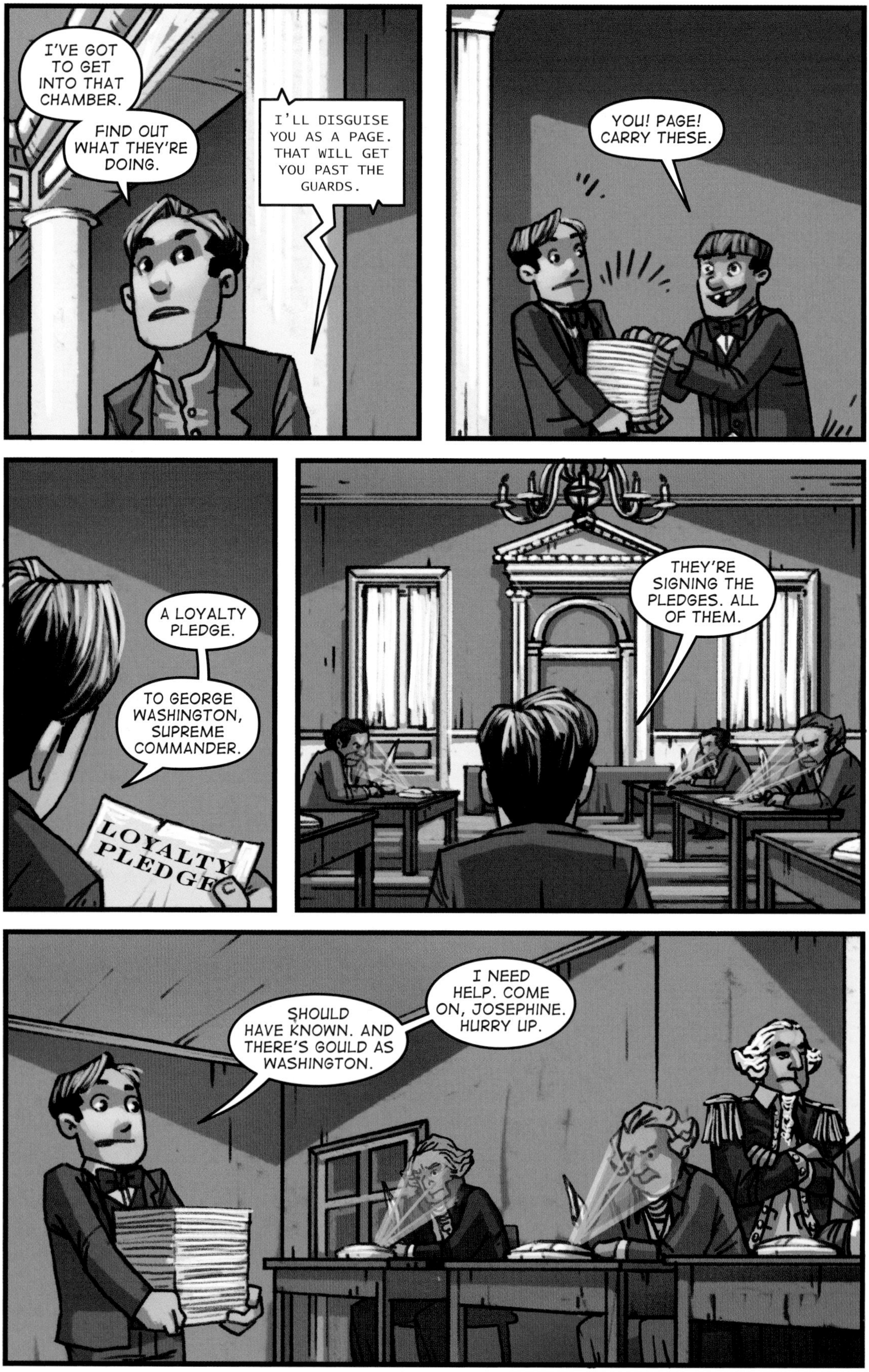
I'VE GOT TO GET INTO THAT CHAMBER.
FIND OUT WHAT THEY'RE DOING.
I'LL DISGUISE YOU AS A PAGE. THAT WILL GET YOU PAST THE GUARDS.
YOU! PAGE! CARRY THESE.
A LOYALTY PLEDGE.
TO GEORGE WASHINGTON, SUPREME COMMANDER.
LOYALTY PLEDGE
THEY'RE SIGNING THE PLEDGES. ALL OF THEM.
SHOULD HAVE KNOWN. AND THERE'S GOULD AS WASHINGTON.
I NEED HELP. COME ON, JOSEPHINE. HURRY UP.

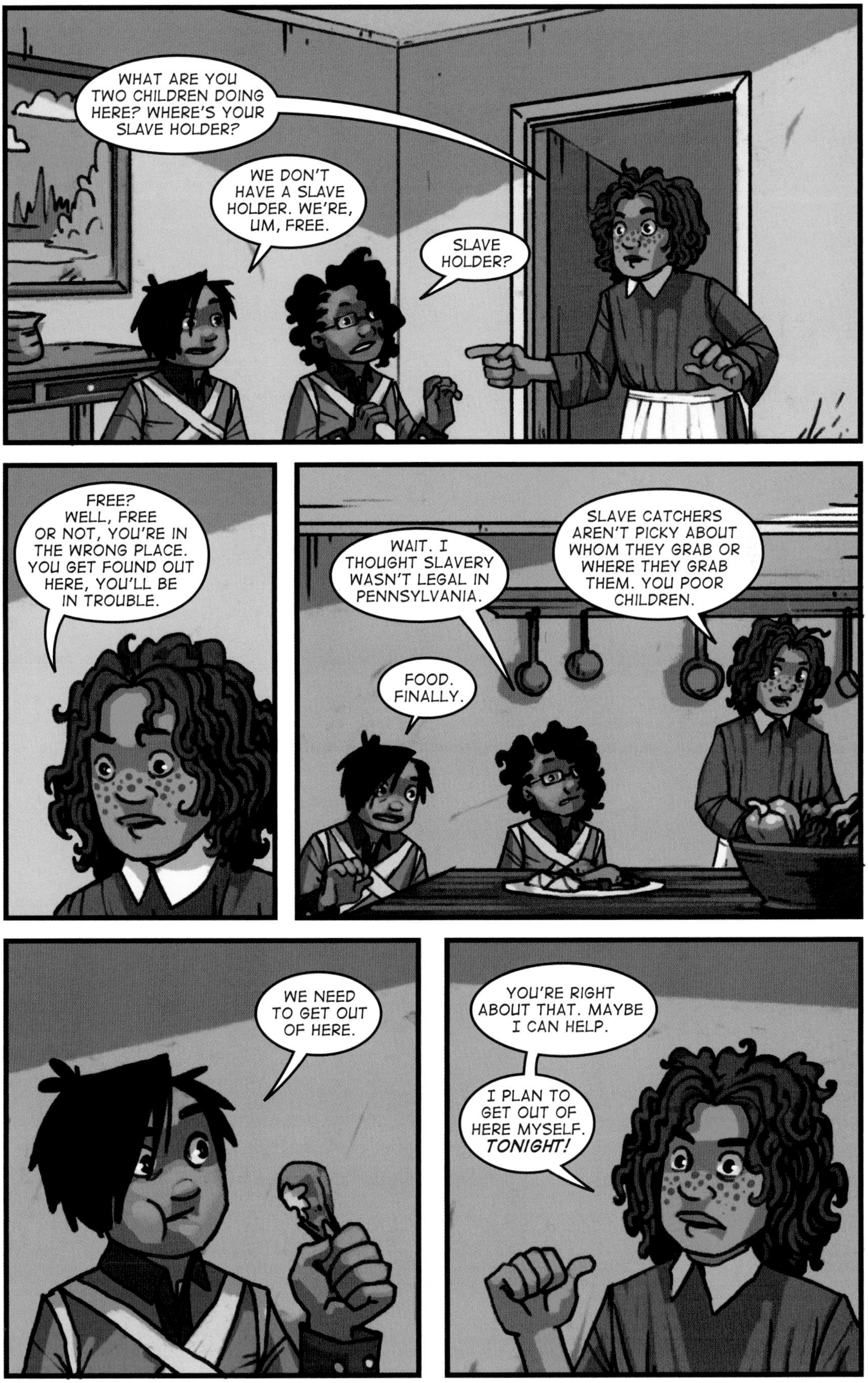

WHAT ARE YOU TWO CHILDREN DOING HERE? WHERE'S YOUR SLAVE HOLDER?
WE DON'T HAVE A SLAVE HOLDER. WE'RE, UM, FREE.
SLAVE HOLDER?
FREE? WELL, FREE OR NOT, YOU'RE IN THE WRONG PLACE. YOU GET FOUND OUT HERE, YOU'LL BE IN TROUBLE.
FOOD. FINALLY.
WAIT. I THOUGHT SLAVERY WASN'T LEGAL IN PENNSYLVANIA.
SLAVE CATCHERS AREN'T PICKY ABOUT WHOM THEY GRAB OR WHERE THEY GRAB THEM. YOU POOR CHILDREN.
WE NEED TO GET OUT OF HERE.
YOU'RE RIGHT ABOUT THAT. MAYBE I CAN HELP.
I PLAN TO GET OUT OF HERE MYSELF. *TONIGHT!*

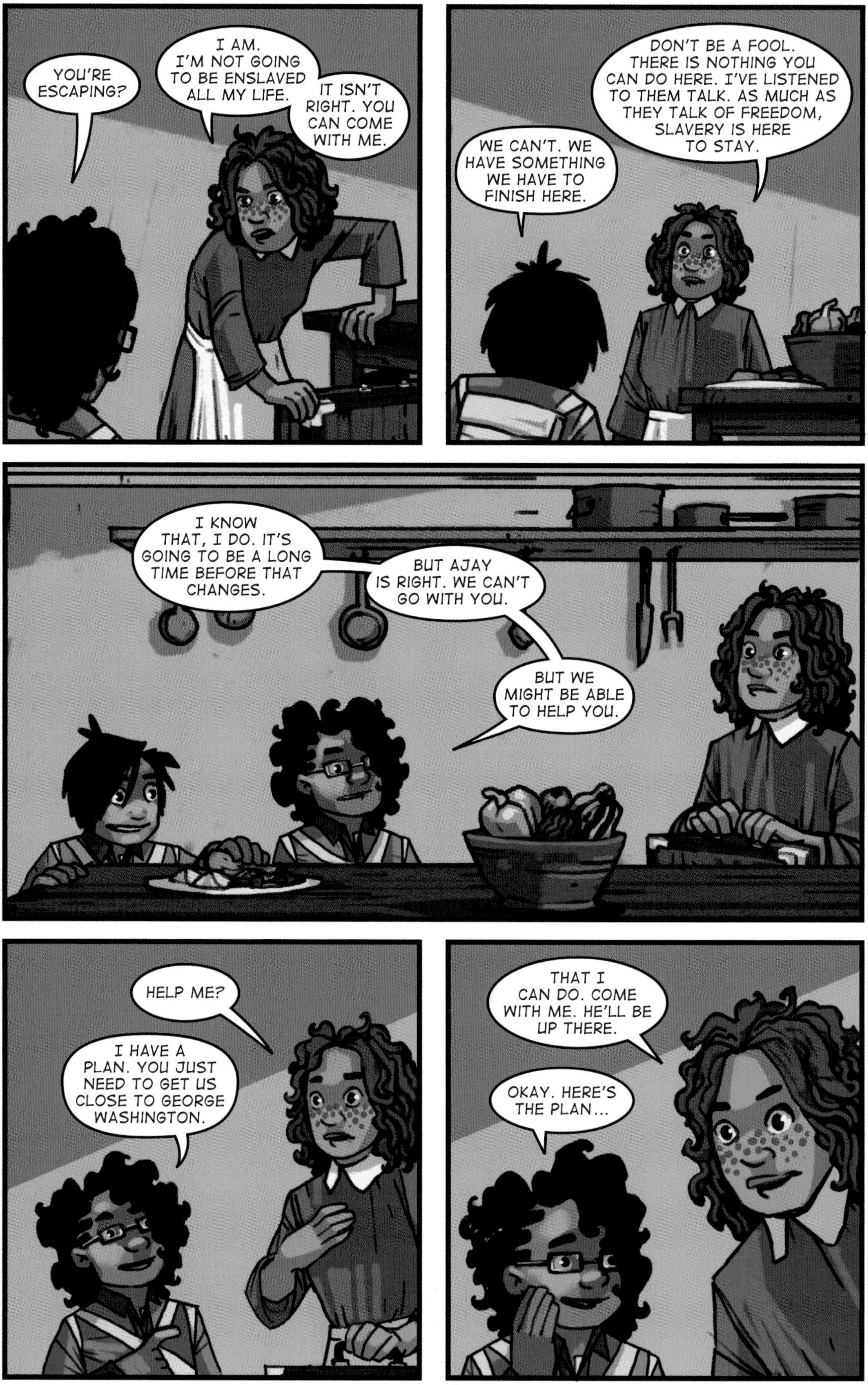
YOU'RE ESCAPING?
I AM. I'M NOT GOING TO BE ENSLAVED ALL MY LIFE.
IT ISN'T RIGHT. YOU CAN COME WITH ME.
WE CAN'T. WE HAVE SOMETHING WE HAVE TO FINISH HERE.
DON'T BE A FOOL. THERE IS NOTHING YOU CAN DO HERE. I'VE LISTENED TO THEM TALK. AS MUCH AS THEY TALK OF FREEDOM, SLAVERY IS HERE TO STAY.
I KNOW THAT, I DO. IT'S GOING TO BE A LONG TIME BEFORE THAT CHANGES.
BUT AJAY IS RIGHT. WE CAN'T GO WITH YOU.
BUT WE MIGHT BE ABLE TO HELP YOU.
HELP ME?
I HAVE A PLAN. YOU JUST NEED TO GET US CLOSE TO GEORGE WASHINGTON.
THAT I CAN DO. COME WITH ME. HE'LL BE UP THERE.
OKAY. HERE'S THE PLAN...

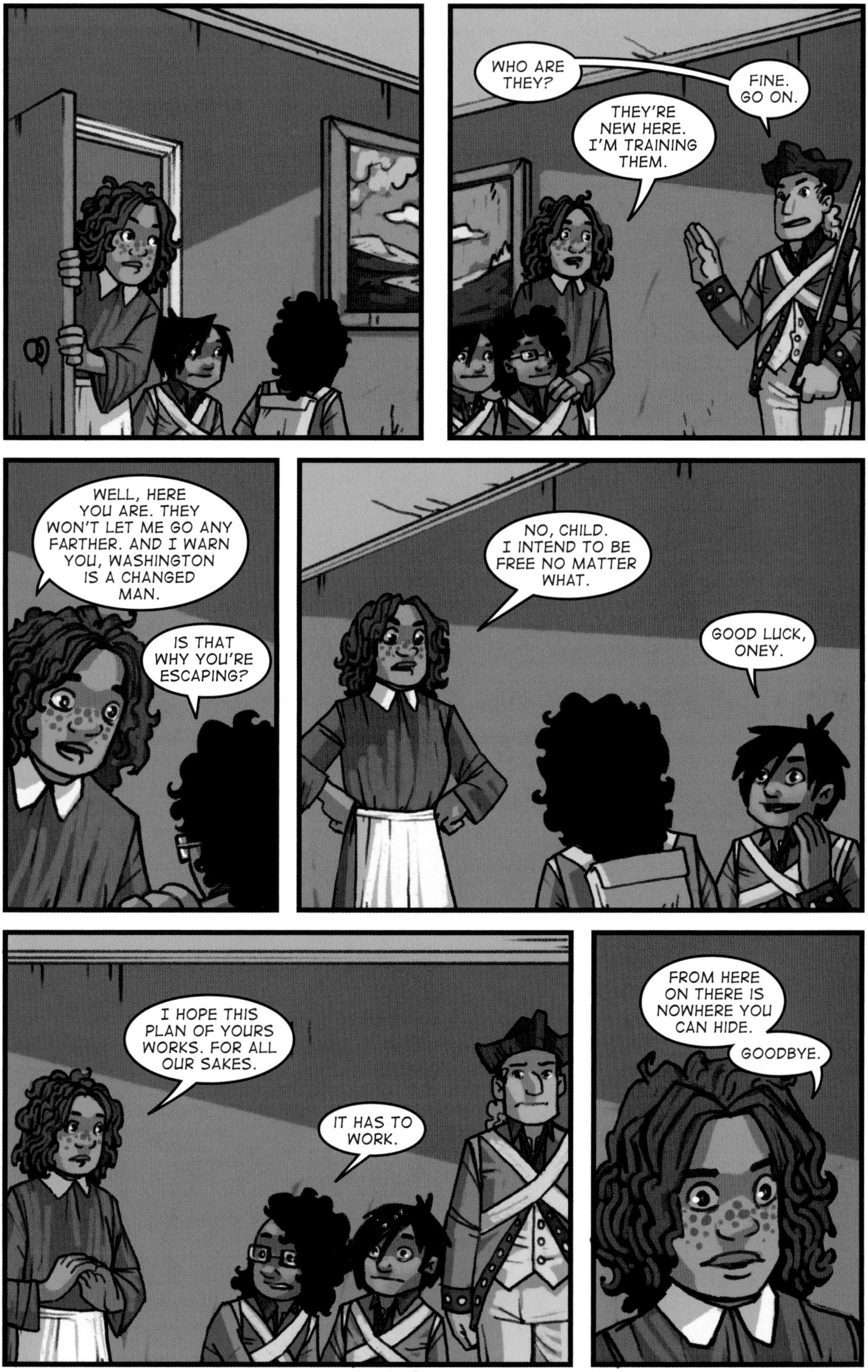
WHO ARE THEY?
FINE. GO ON.
THEY'RE NEW HERE. I'M TRAINING THEM.
WELL, HERE YOU ARE. THEY WON'T LET ME GO ANY FARTHER. AND I WARN YOU, WASHINGTON IS A CHANGED MAN.
IS THAT WHY YOU'RE ESCAPING?
NO, CHILD. I INTEND TO BE FREE NO MATTER WHAT.
GOOD LUCK, ONEY.
I HOPE THIS PLAN OF YOURS WORKS. FOR ALL OUR SAKES.
IT HAS TO WORK.
FROM HERE ON THERE IS NOWHERE YOU CAN HIDE.
GOODBYE.

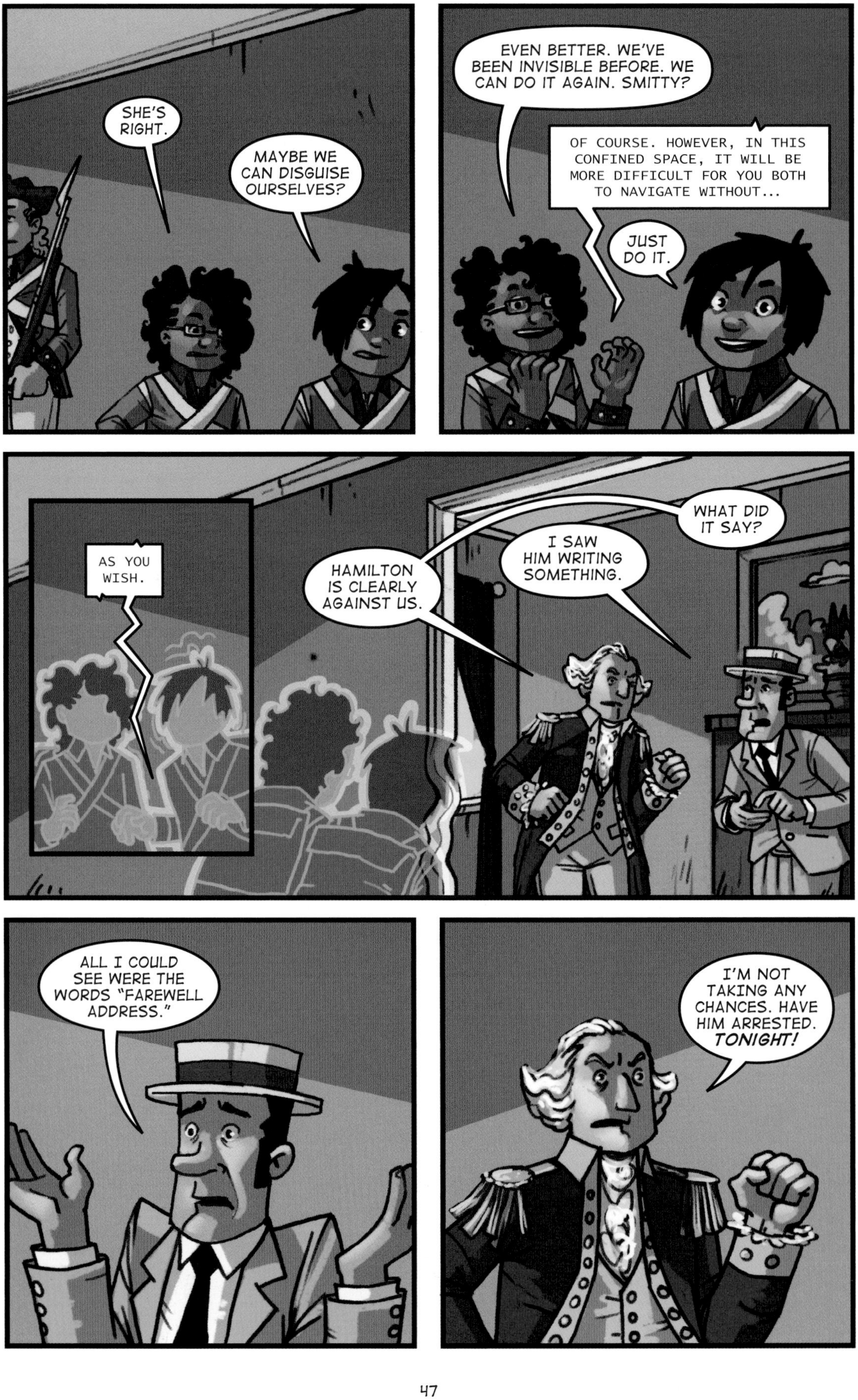
SHE'S RIGHT.
MAYBE WE CAN DISGUISE OURSELVES?
EVEN BETTER. WE'VE BEEN INVISIBLE BEFORE. WE CAN DO IT AGAIN. SMITTY?
OF COURSE. HOWEVER, IN THIS CONFINED SPACE, IT WILL BE MORE DIFFICULT FOR YOU BOTH TO NAVIGATE WITHOUT...
JUST DO IT.
AS YOU WISH.
HAMILTON IS CLEARLY AGAINST US.
I SAW HIM WRITING SOMETHING.
WHAT DID IT SAY?
ALL I COULD SEE WERE THE WORDS "FAREWELL ADDRESS."
I'M NOT TAKING ANY CHANCES. HAVE HIM ARRESTED. *TONIGHT!*

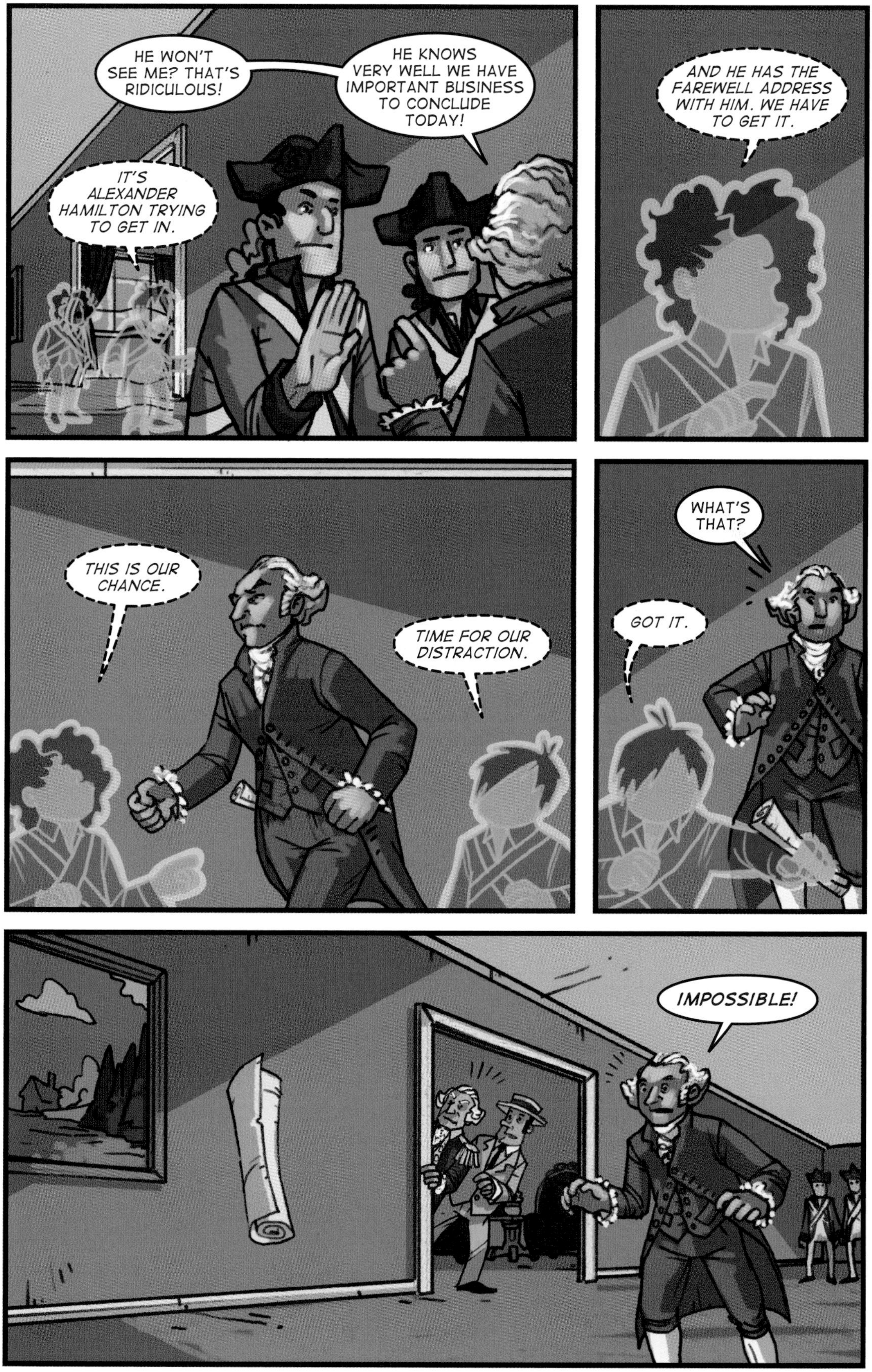
HE WON'T SEE ME? THAT'S RIDICULOUS!
HE KNOWS VERY WELL WE HAVE IMPORTANT BUSINESS TO CONCLUDE TODAY!
IT'S ALEXANDER HAMILTON TRYING TO GET IN.
AND HE HAS THE FAREWELL ADDRESS WITH HIM. WE HAVE TO GET IT.
THIS IS OUR CHANCE.
TIME FOR OUR DISTRACTION.
WHAT'S THAT?
GOT IT.
IMPOSSIBLE!

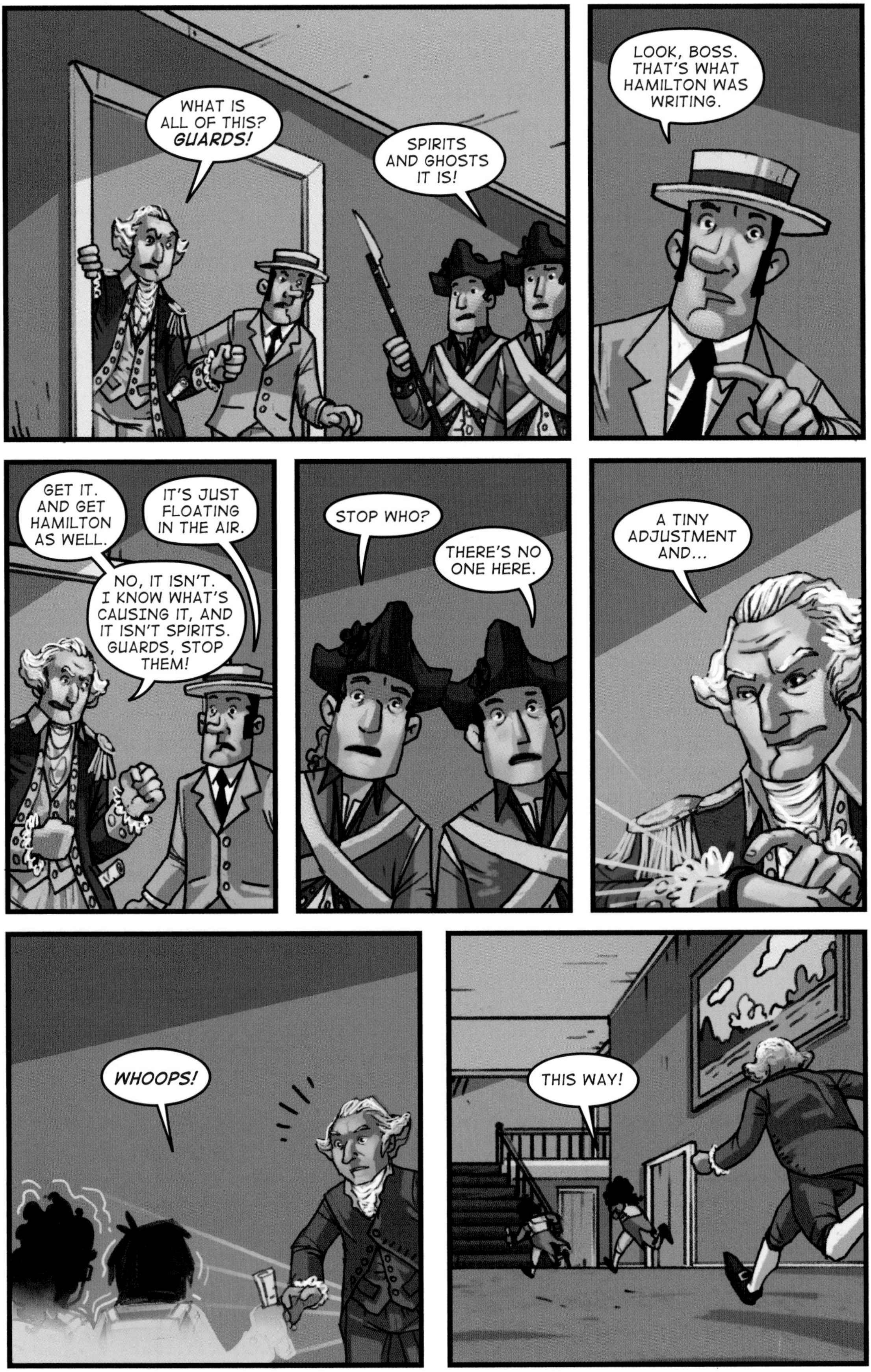
WHAT IS ALL OF THIS? GUARDS!
SPIRITS AND GHOSTS IT IS!
LOOK, BOSS. THAT'S WHAT HAMILTON WAS WRITING.
GET IT. AND GET HAMILTON AS WELL.
IT'S JUST FLOATING IN THE AIR.
NO, IT ISN'T. I KNOW WHAT'S CAUSING IT, AND IT ISN'T SPIRITS. GUARDS, STOP THEM!
STOP WHO?
THERE'S NO ONE HERE.
A TINY ADJUSTMENT AND...
WHOOPS!
THIS WAY!

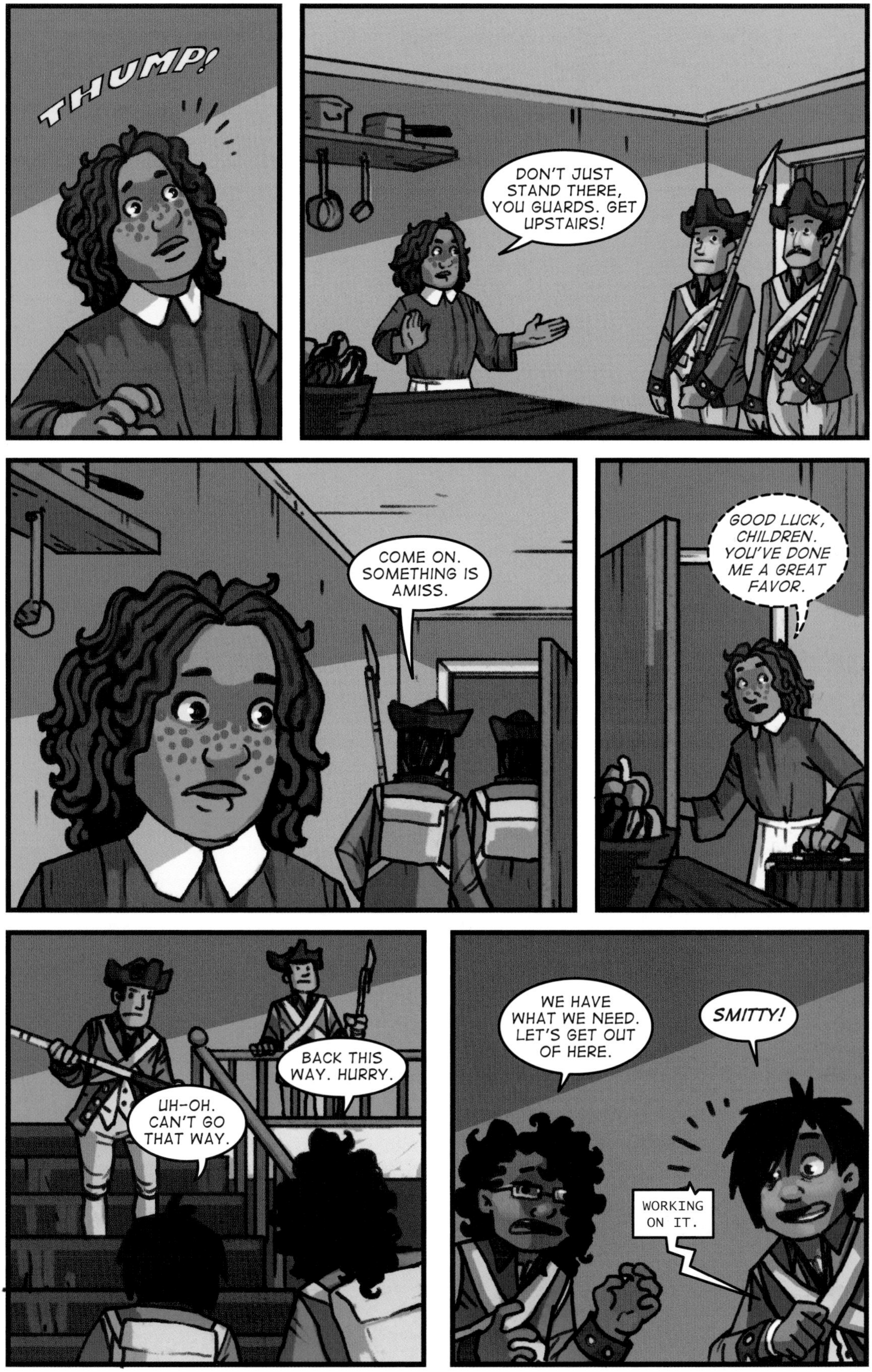
THUMP!
DON'T JUST STAND THERE, YOU GUARDS. GET UPSTAIRS!
COME ON. SOMETHING IS AMISS.
GOOD LUCK, CHILDREN. YOU'VE DONE ME A GREAT FAVOR.
BACK THIS WAY. HURRY.
UH-OH. CAN'T GO THAT WAY.
WE HAVE WHAT WE NEED. LET'S GET OUT OF HERE.
SMITTY!
WORKING ON IT.

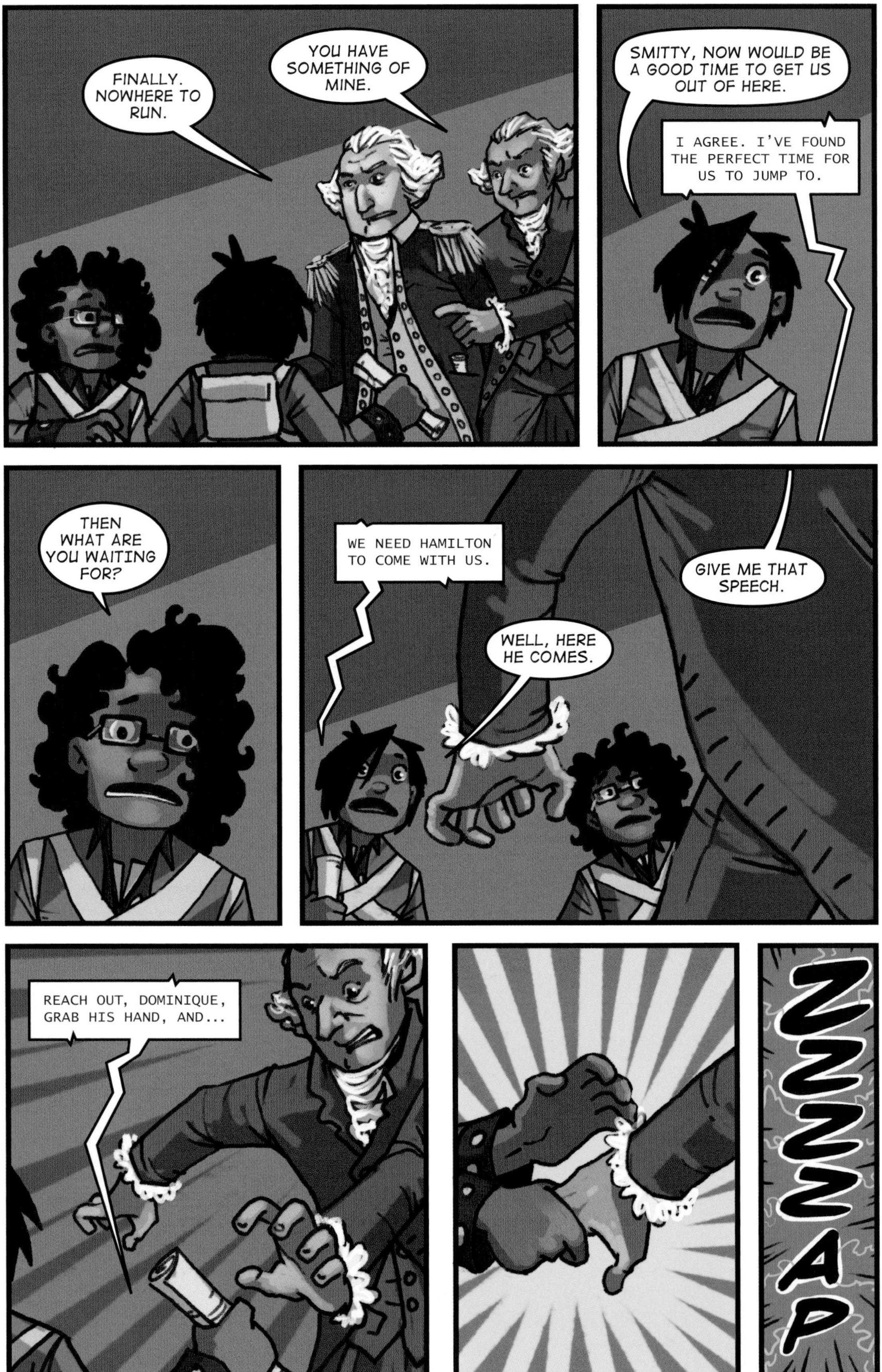
FINALLY. NOWHERE TO RUN.
YOU HAVE SOMETHING OF MINE.
SMITTY, NOW WOULD BE A GOOD TIME TO GET US OUT OF HERE.
I AGREE. I'VE FOUND THE PERFECT TIME FOR US TO JUMP TO.
THEN WHAT ARE YOU WAITING FOR?
WE NEED HAMILTON TO COME WITH US.
GIVE ME THAT SPEECH.
WELL, HERE HE COMES.
REACH OUT, DOMINIQUE, GRAB HIS HAND, AND...
ZZZZAP

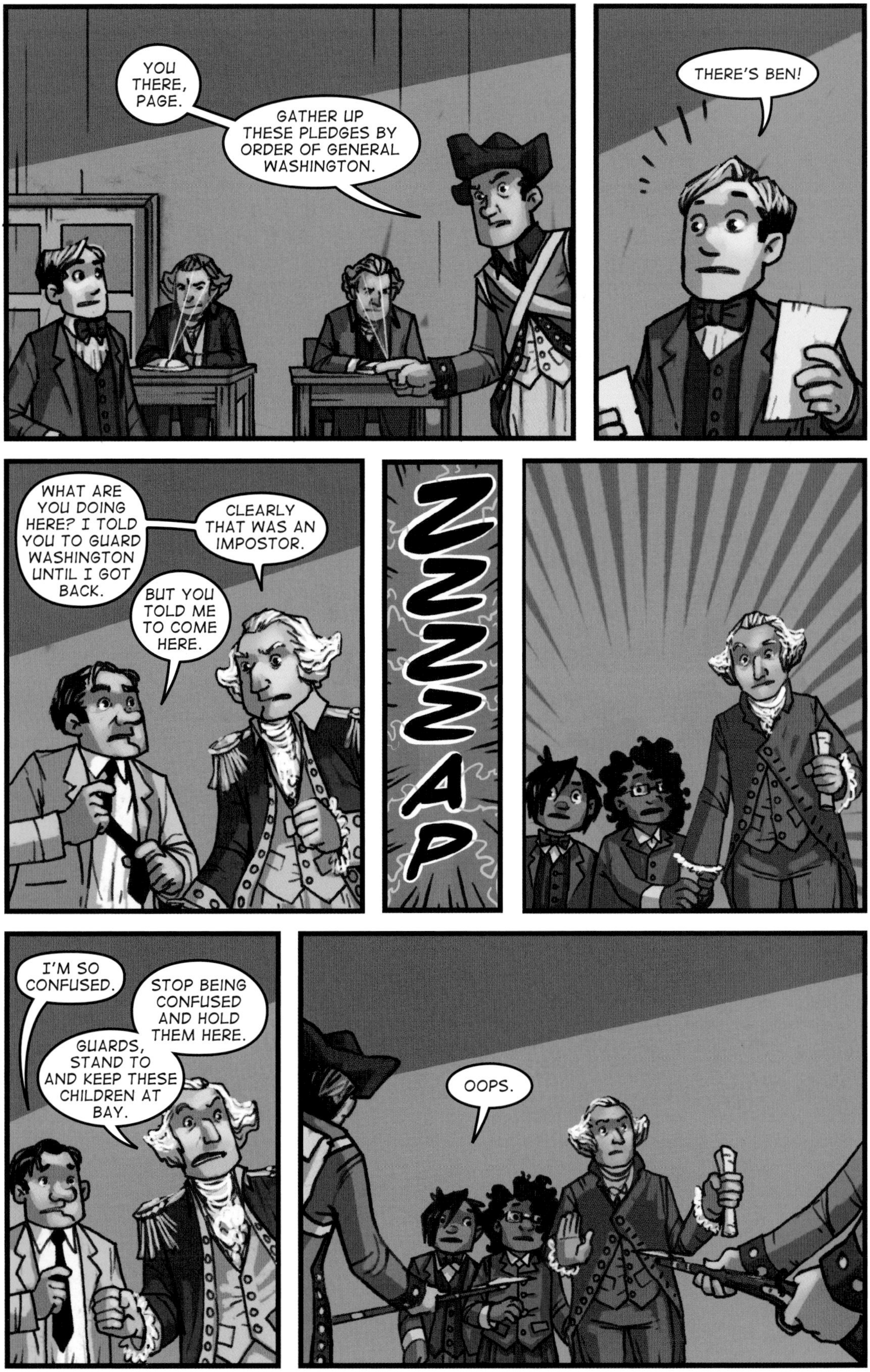
YOU THERE, PAGE.
GATHER UP THESE PLEDGES BY ORDER OF GENERAL WASHINGTON.
THERE'S BEN!
WHAT ARE YOU DOING HERE? I TOLD YOU TO GUARD WASHINGTON UNTIL I GOT BACK.
CLEARLY THAT WAS AN IMPOSTOR.
BUT YOU TOLD ME TO COME HERE.
ZZZZAP
I'M SO CONFUSED.
STOP BEING CONFUSED AND HOLD THEM HERE.
GUARDS, STAND TO AND KEEP THESE CHILDREN AT BAY.
OOPS.

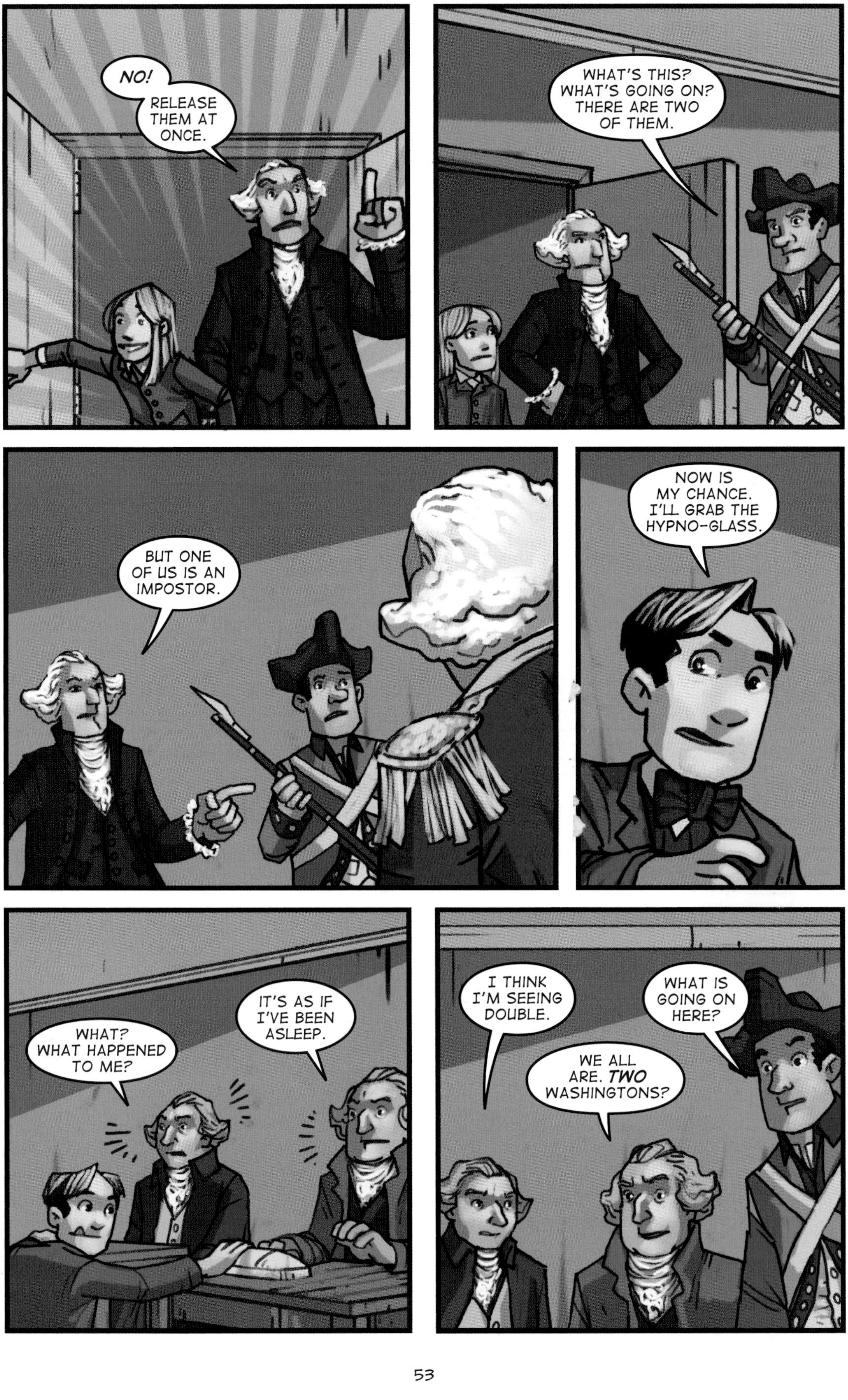
NO! RELEASE THEM AT ONCE.
WHAT'S THIS? WHAT'S GOING ON? THERE ARE TWO OF THEM.
BUT ONE OF US IS AN IMPOSTOR.
NOW IS MY CHANCE. I'LL GRAB THE HYPNO-GLASS.
WHAT? WHAT HAPPENED TO ME?
IT'S AS IF I'VE BEEN ASLEEP.
I THINK I'M SEEING DOUBLE.
WHAT IS GOING ON HERE?
WE ALL ARE. ***TWO*** WASHINGTONS?

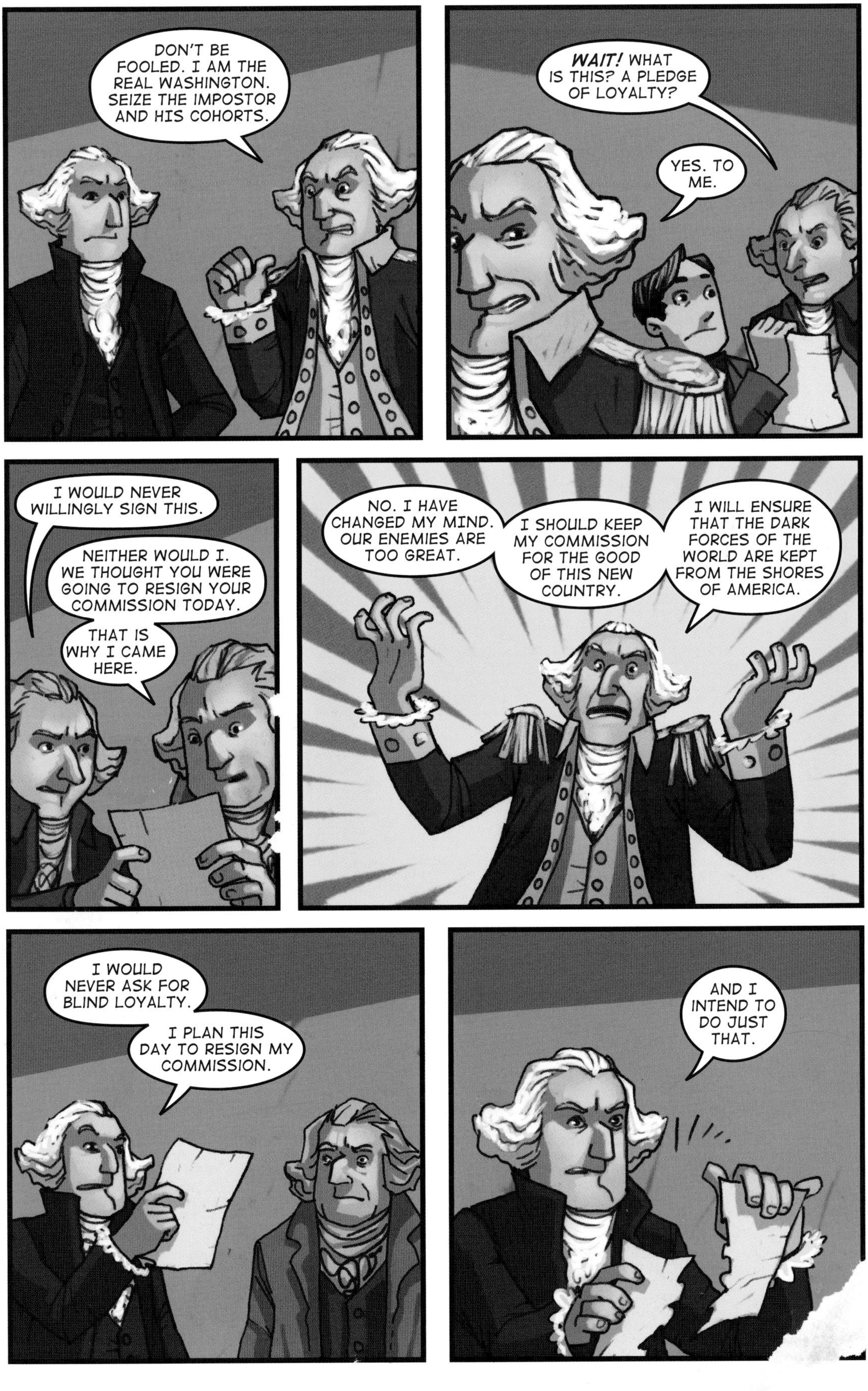
DON'T BE FOOLED. I AM THE REAL WASHINGTON. SEIZE THE IMPOSTOR AND HIS COHORTS.
WAIT! WHAT IS THIS? A PLEDGE OF LOYALTY?
YES. TO ME.
I WOULD NEVER WILLINGLY SIGN THIS.
NEITHER WOULD I. WE THOUGHT YOU WERE GOING TO RESIGN YOUR COMMISSION TODAY.
THAT IS WHY I CAME HERE.
NO. I HAVE CHANGED MY MIND. OUR ENEMIES ARE TOO GREAT.
I SHOULD KEEP MY COMMISSION FOR THE GOOD OF THIS NEW COUNTRY.
I WILL ENSURE THAT THE DARK FORCES OF THE WORLD ARE KEPT FROM THE SHORES OF AMERICA.
I WOULD NEVER ASK FOR BLIND LOYALTY.
I PLAN THIS DAY TO RESIGN MY COMMISSION.
AND I INTEND TO DO JUST THAT.

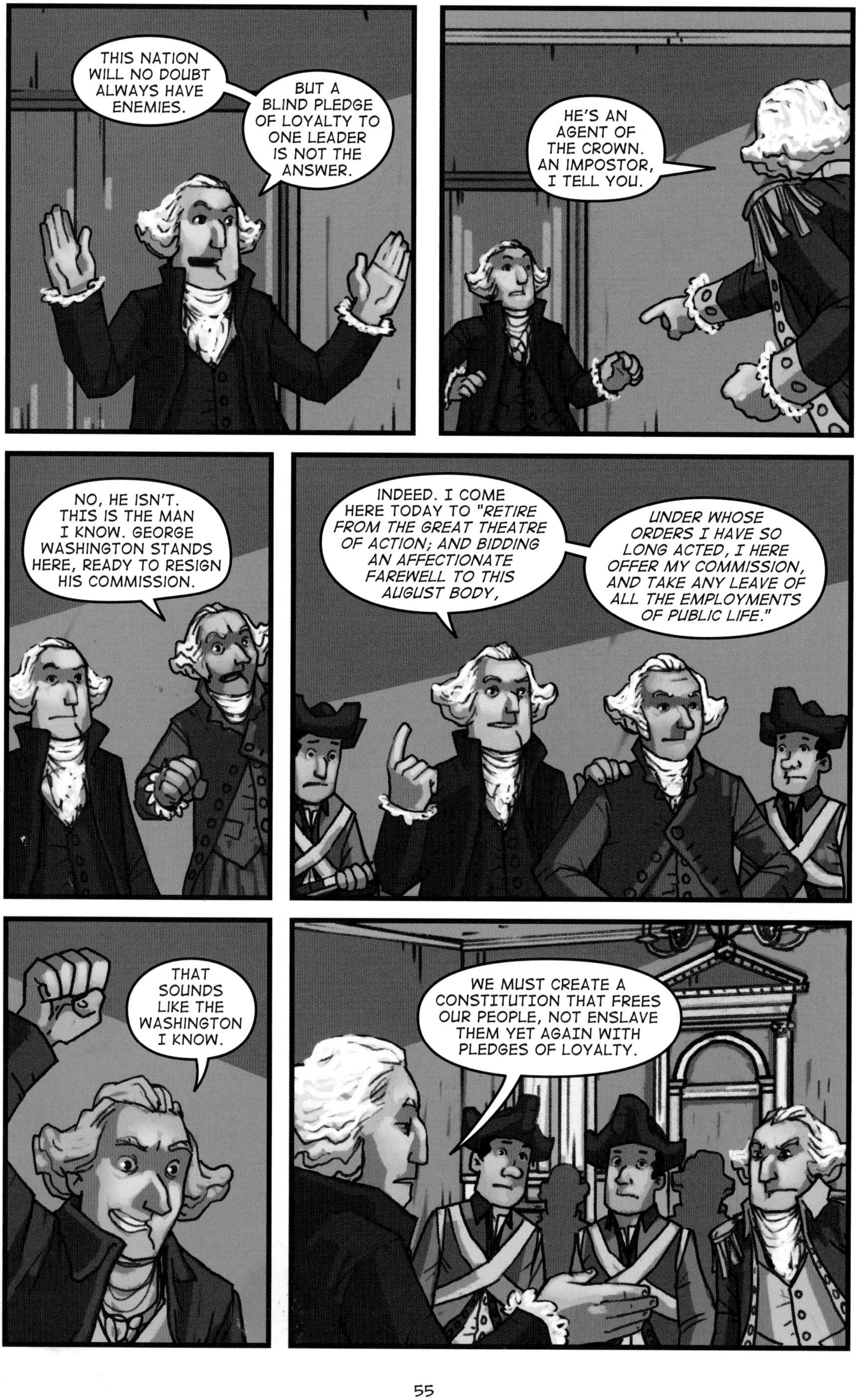
THIS NATION WILL NO DOUBT ALWAYS HAVE ENEMIES.
BUT A BLIND PLEDGE OF LOYALTY TO ONE LEADER IS NOT THE ANSWER.
HE'S AN AGENT OF THE CROWN. AN IMPOSTOR, I TELL YOU.
NO, HE ISN'T. THIS IS THE MAN I KNOW. GEORGE WASHINGTON STANDS HERE, READY TO RESIGN HIS COMMISSION.
INDEED. I COME HERE TODAY TO "RETIRE FROM THE GREAT THEATRE OF ACTION; AND BIDDING AN AFFECTIONATE FAREWELL TO THIS AUGUST BODY,
UNDER WHOSE ORDERS I HAVE SO LONG ACTED, I HERE OFFER MY COMMISSION, AND TAKE ANY LEAVE OF ALL THE EMPLOYMENTS OF PUBLIC LIFE."
THAT SOUNDS LIKE THE WASHINGTON I KNOW.
WE MUST CREATE A CONSTITUTION THAT FREES OUR PEOPLE, NOT ENSLAVE THEM YET AGAIN WITH PLEDGES OF LOYALTY.

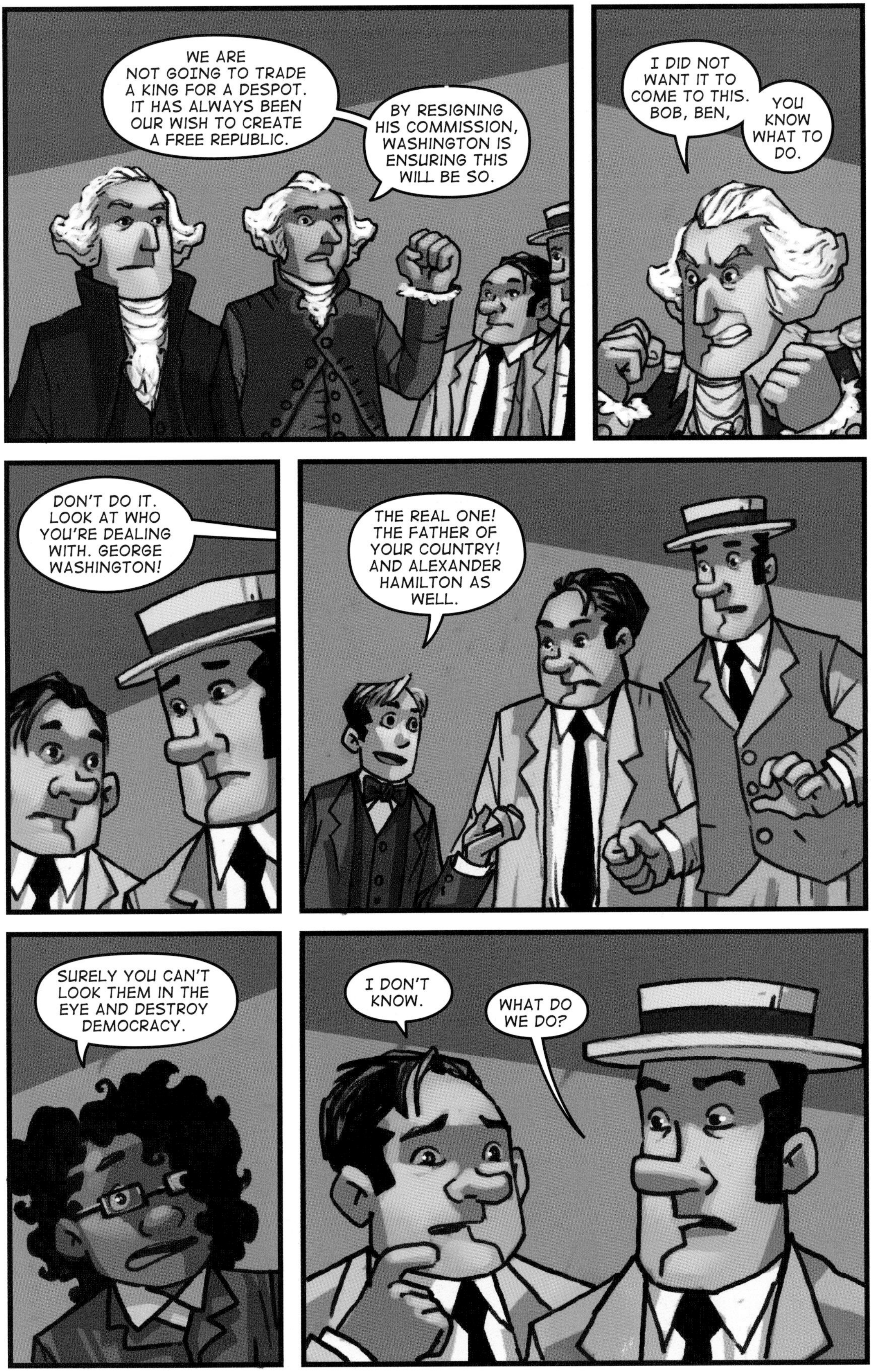
WE ARE NOT GOING TO TRADE A KING FOR A DESPOT. IT HAS ALWAYS BEEN OUR WISH TO CREATE A FREE REPUBLIC.
BY RESIGNING HIS COMMISSION, WASHINGTON IS ENSURING THIS WILL BE SO.
I DID NOT WANT IT TO COME TO THIS. BOB, BEN,
YOU KNOW WHAT TO DO.
DON'T DO IT. LOOK AT WHO YOU'RE DEALING WITH. GEORGE WASHINGTON!
THE REAL ONE! THE FATHER OF YOUR COUNTRY! AND ALEXANDER HAMILTON AS WELL.
SURELY YOU CAN'T LOOK THEM IN THE EYE AND DESTROY DEMOCRACY.
I DON'T KNOW.
WHAT DO WE DO?

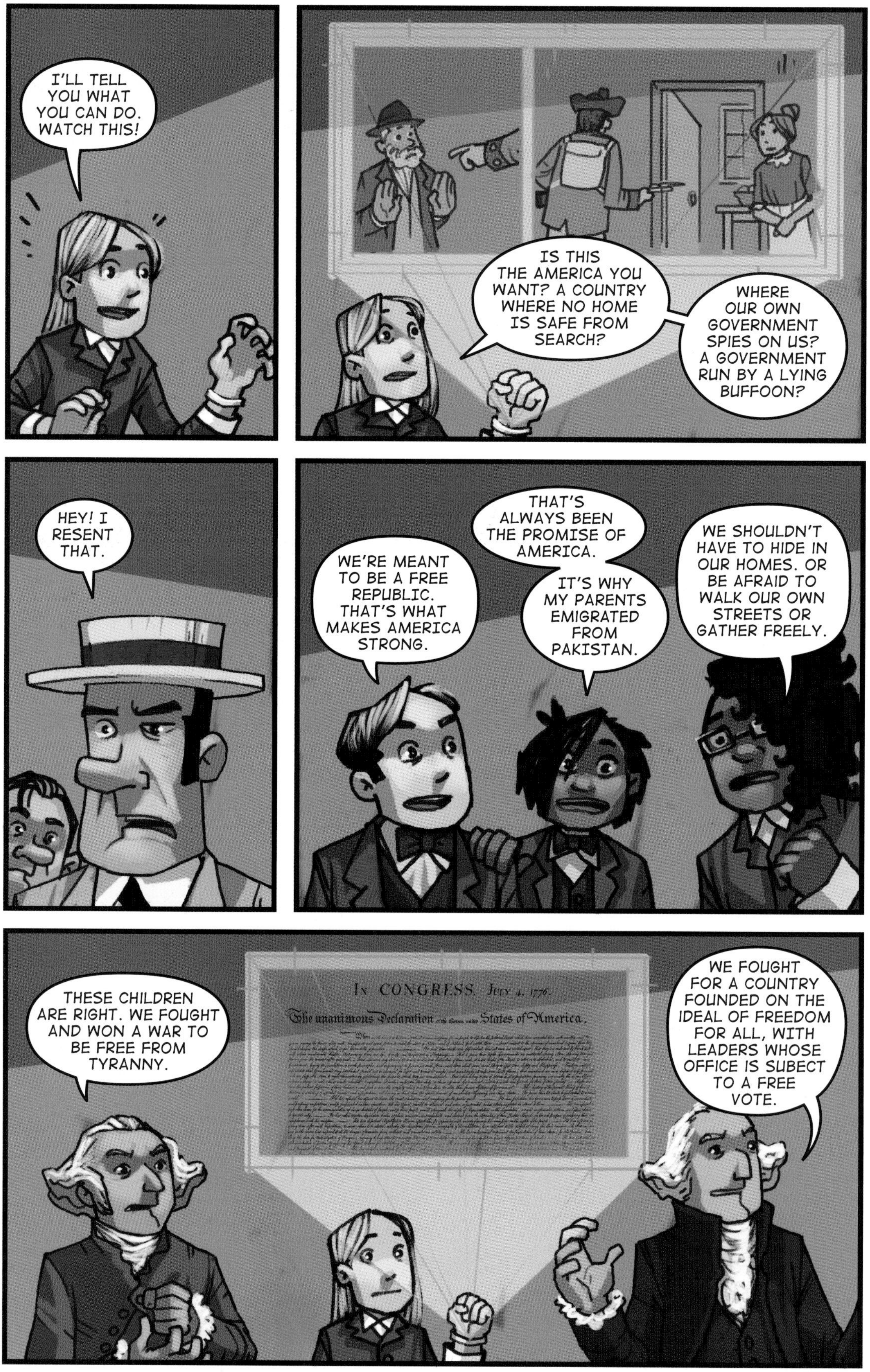
I'LL TELL YOU WHAT YOU CAN DO. WATCH THIS!
IS THIS THE AMERICA YOU WANT? A COUNTRY WHERE NO HOME IS SAFE FROM SEARCH?
WHERE OUR OWN GOVERNMENT SPIES ON US? A GOVERNMENT RUN BY A LYING BUFFOON?
HEY! I RESENT THAT.
WE'RE MEANT TO BE A FREE REPUBLIC. THAT'S WHAT MAKES AMERICA STRONG.
THAT'S ALWAYS BEEN THE PROMISE OF AMERICA.
IT'S WHY MY PARENTS EMIGRATED FROM PAKISTAN.
WE SHOULDN'T HAVE TO HIDE IN OUR HOMES. OR BE AFRAID TO WALK OUR OWN STREETS OR GATHER FREELY.
THESE CHILDREN ARE RIGHT. WE FOUGHT AND WON A WAR TO BE FREE FROM TYRANNY.
IN CONGRESS. JULY 4, 1776.
WE FOUGHT FOR A COUNTRY FOUNDED ON THE IDEAL OF FREEDOM FOR ALL, WITH LEADERS WHOSE OFFICE IS SUBECT TO A FREE VOTE.

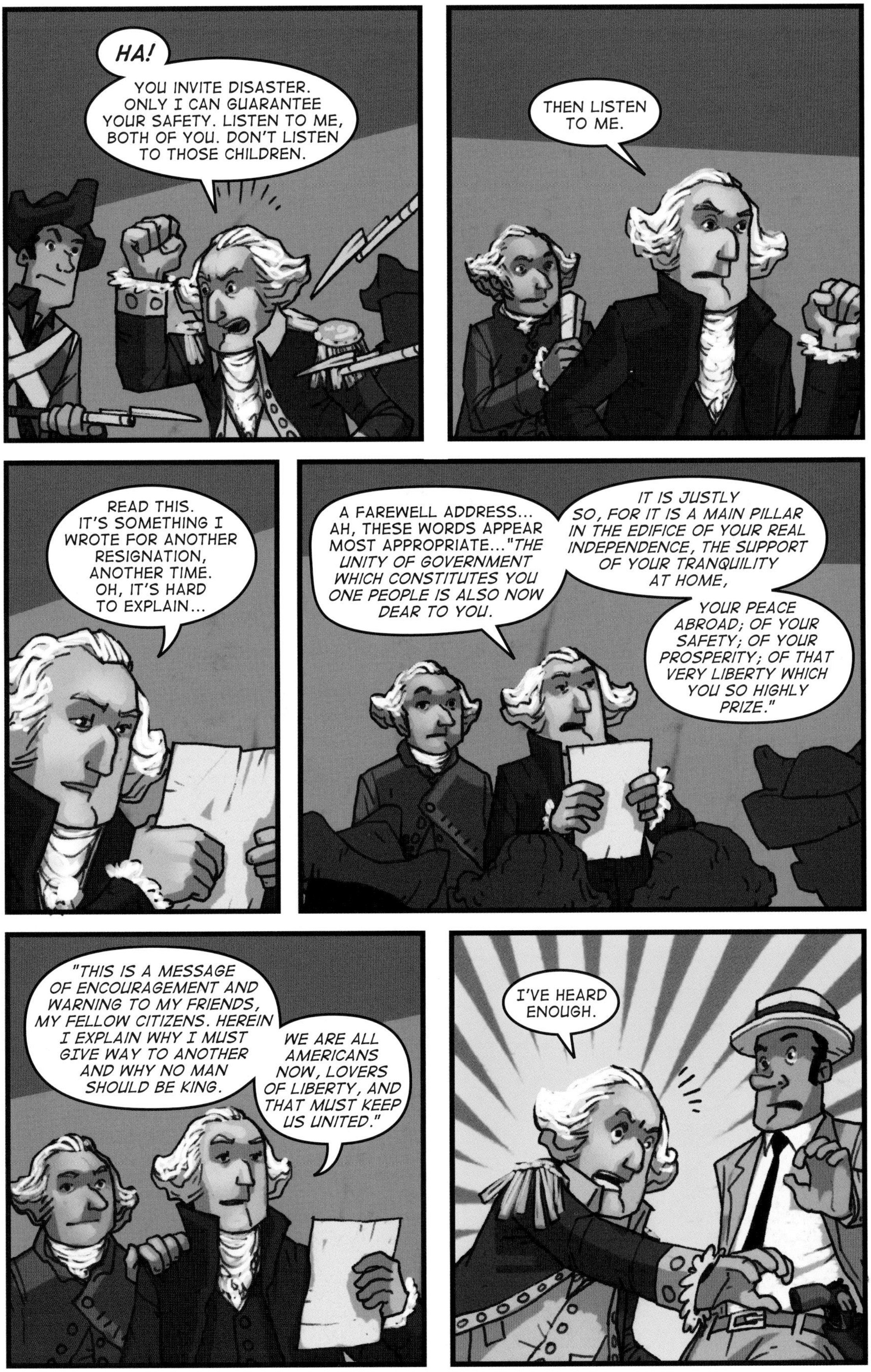
HA!
YOU INVITE DISASTER. ONLY I CAN GUARANTEE YOUR SAFETY. LISTEN TO ME, BOTH OF YOU. DON'T LISTEN TO THOSE CHILDREN.
THEN LISTEN TO ME.
READ THIS. IT'S SOMETHING I WROTE FOR ANOTHER RESIGNATION, ANOTHER TIME. OH, IT'S HARD TO EXPLAIN...
A FAREWELL ADDRESS... AH, THESE WORDS APPEAR MOST APPROPRIATE..."THE UNITY OF GOVERNMENT WHICH CONSTITUTES YOU ONE PEOPLE IS ALSO NOW DEAR TO YOU.
IT IS JUSTLY SO, FOR IT IS A MAIN PILLAR IN THE EDIFICE OF YOUR REAL INDEPENDENCE, THE SUPPORT OF YOUR TRANQUILITY AT HOME,
YOUR PEACE ABROAD; OF YOUR SAFETY; OF YOUR PROSPERITY; OF THAT VERY LIBERTY WHICH YOU SO HIGHLY PRIZE."
"THIS IS A MESSAGE OF ENCOURAGEMENT AND WARNING TO MY FRIENDS, MY FELLOW CITIZENS. HEREIN I EXPLAIN WHY I MUST GIVE WAY TO ANOTHER AND WHY NO MAN SHOULD BE KING.
WE ARE ALL AMERICANS NOW, LOVERS OF LIBERTY, AND THAT MUST KEEP US UNITED."
I'VE HEARD ENOUGH.

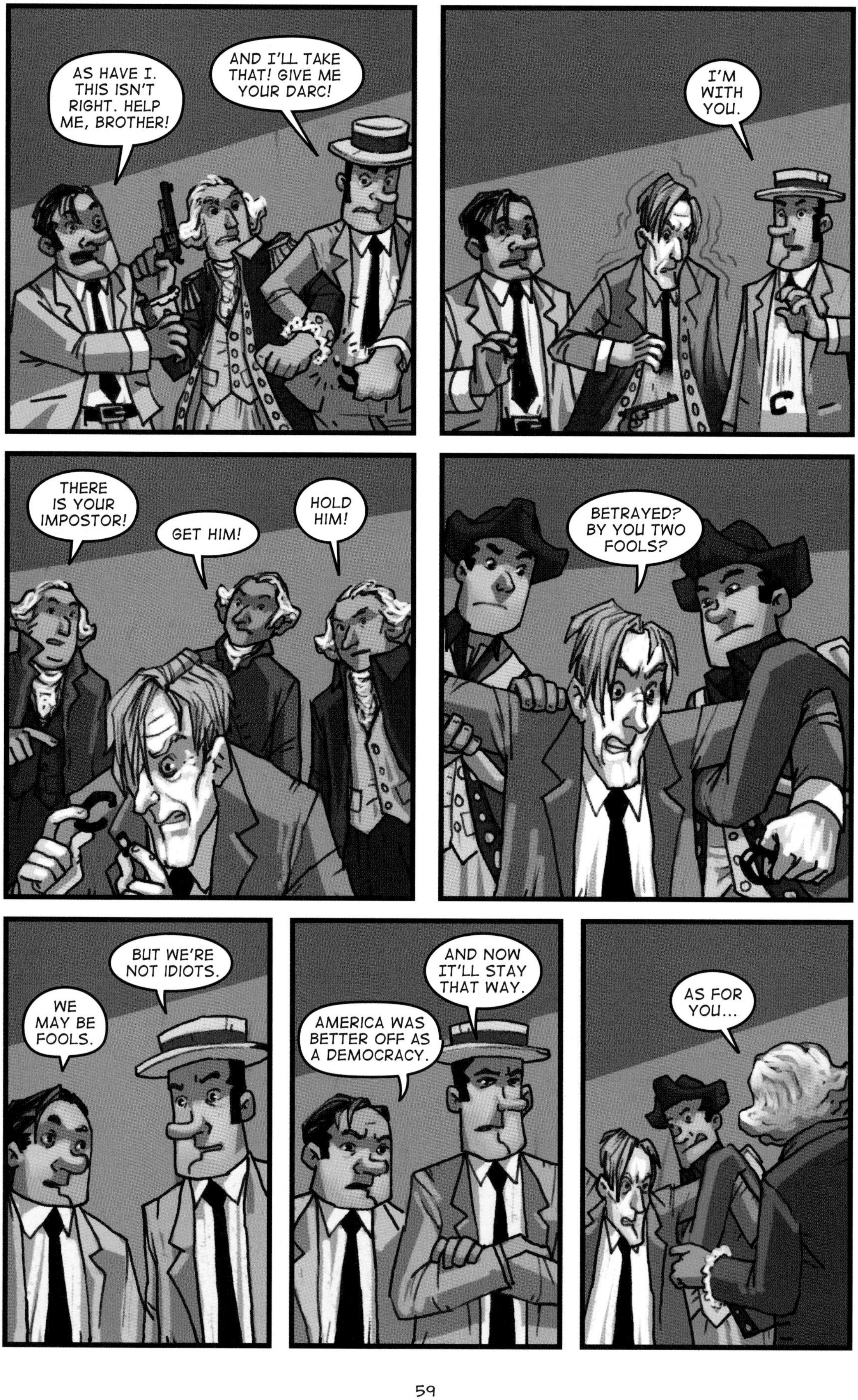
AS HAVE I. THIS ISN'T RIGHT. HELP ME, BROTHER!
AND I'LL TAKE THAT! GIVE ME YOUR DARC!
I'M WITH YOU.
THERE IS YOUR IMPOSTOR!
GET HIM!
HOLD HIM!
BETRAYED? BY YOU TWO FOOLS?
WE MAY BE FOOLS.
BUT WE'RE NOT IDIOTS.
AMERICA WAS BETTER OFF AS A DEMOCRACY.
AND NOW IT'LL STAY THAT WAY.
AS FOR YOU...

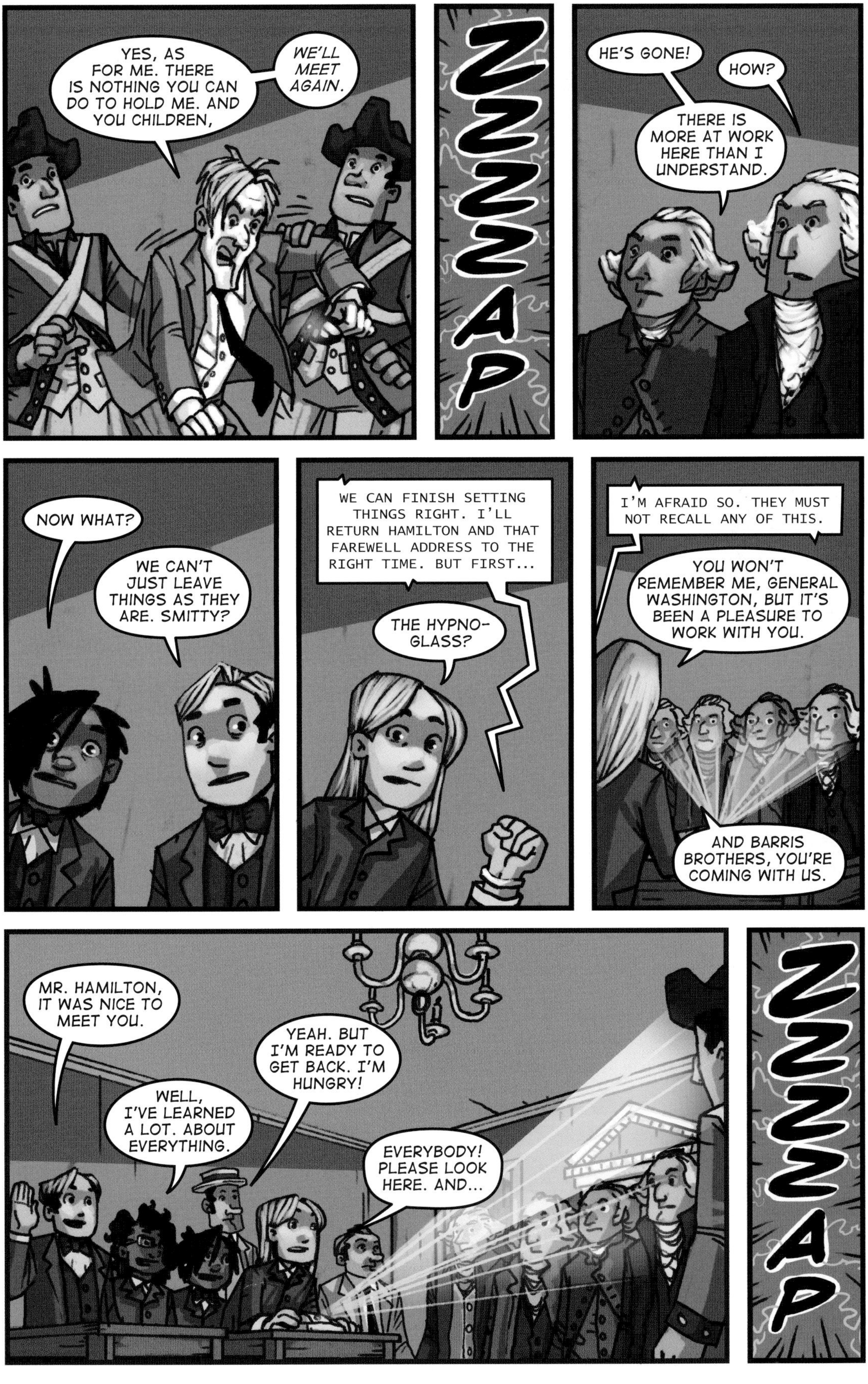
YES, AS FOR ME. THERE IS NOTHING YOU CAN DO TO HOLD ME. AND YOU CHILDREN,
WE'LL MEET AGAIN.
ZZZZAP
HE'S GONE!
HOW?
THERE IS MORE AT WORK HERE THAN I UNDERSTAND.
NOW WHAT?
WE CAN'T JUST LEAVE THINGS AS THEY ARE. SMITTY?
WE CAN FINISH SETTING THINGS RIGHT. I'LL RETURN HAMILTON AND THAT FAREWELL ADDRESS TO THE RIGHT TIME. BUT FIRST...
THE HYPNO-GLASS?
I'M AFRAID SO. THEY MUST NOT RECALL ANY OF THIS.
YOU WON'T REMEMBER ME, GENERAL WASHINGTON, BUT IT'S BEEN A PLEASURE TO WORK WITH YOU.
AND BARRIS BROTHERS, YOU'RE COMING WITH US.
MR. HAMILTON, IT WAS NICE TO MEET YOU.
WELL, I'VE LEARNED A LOT. ABOUT EVERYTHING.
YEAH. BUT I'M READY TO GET BACK. I'M HUNGRY!
EVERYBODY! PLEASE LOOK HERE. AND...
ZZZZAP

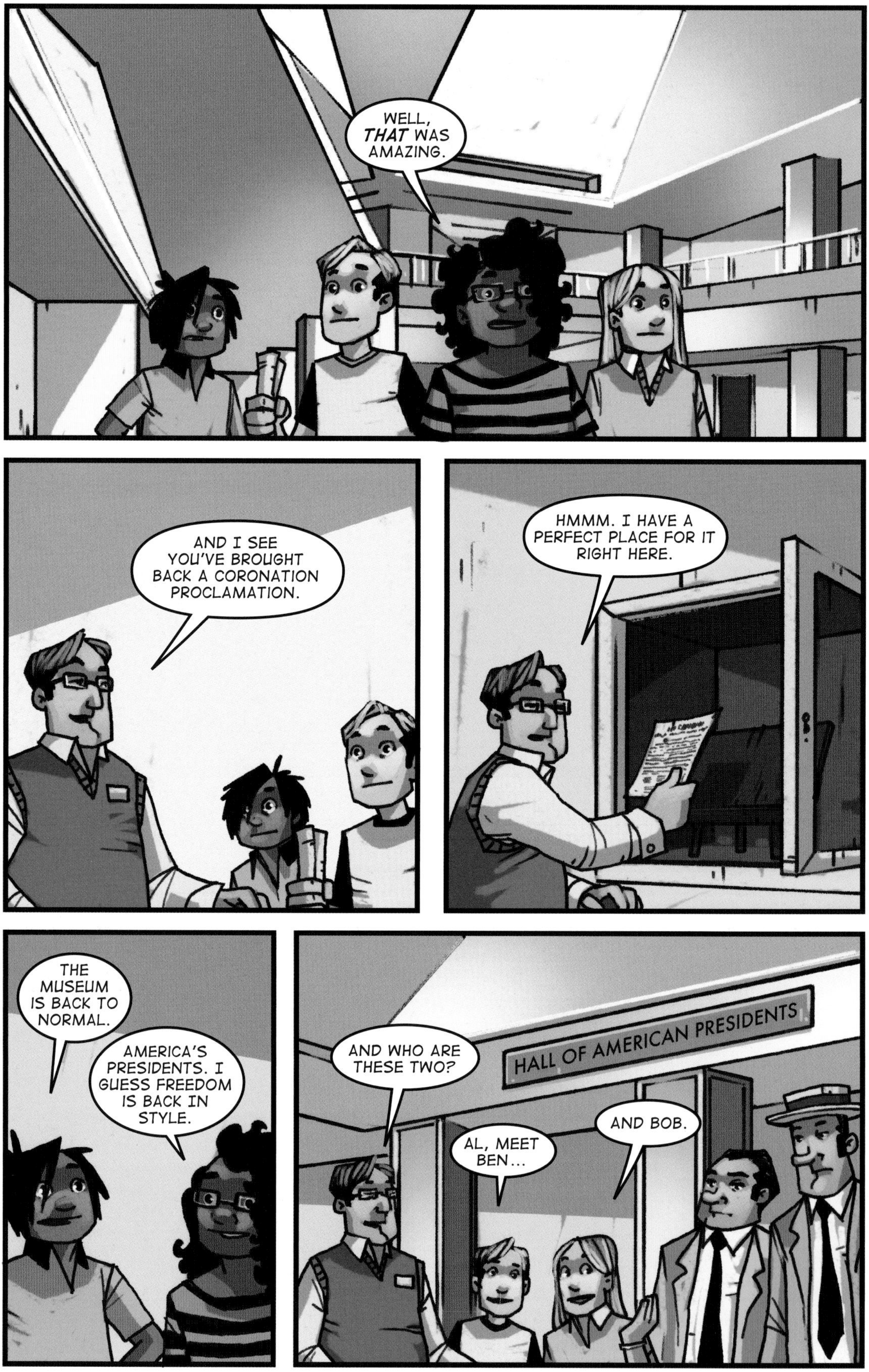
WELL, *THAT* WAS AMAZING.
AND I SEE YOU'VE BROUGHT BACK A CORONATION PROCLAMATION.
HMMM. I HAVE A PERFECT PLACE FOR IT RIGHT HERE.
THE MUSEUM IS BACK TO NORMAL.
AMERICA'S PRESIDENTS. I GUESS FREEDOM IS BACK IN STYLE.
HALL OF AMERICAN PRESIDENTS
AND WHO ARE THESE TWO?
AL, MEET BEN...
AND BOB.

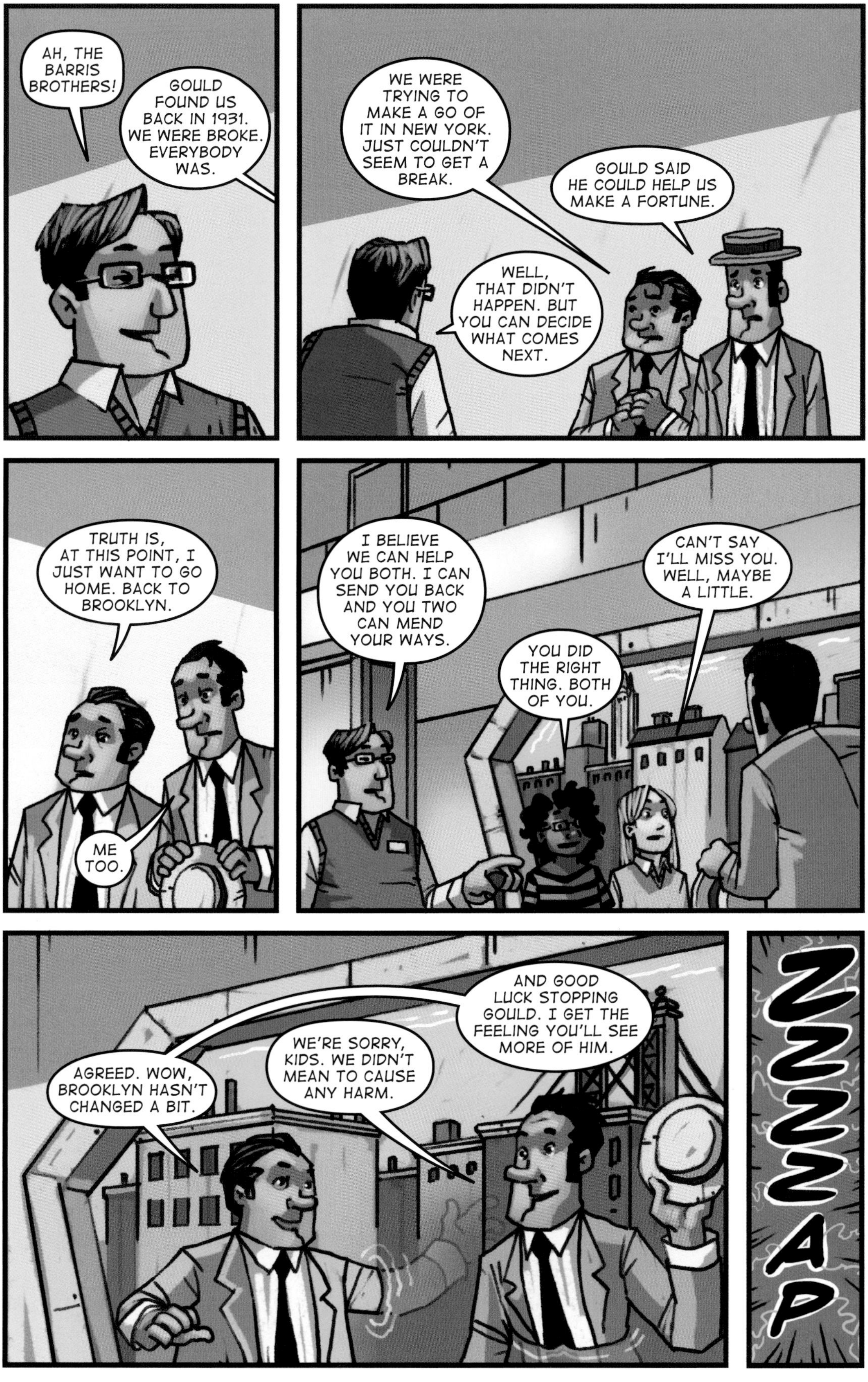
AH, THE BARRIS BROTHERS!
GOULD FOUND US BACK IN 1931. WE WERE BROKE. EVERYBODY WAS.
WE WERE TRYING TO MAKE A GO OF IT IN NEW YORK. JUST COULDN'T SEEM TO GET A BREAK.
GOULD SAID HE COULD HELP US MAKE A FORTUNE.
WELL, THAT DIDN'T HAPPEN. BUT YOU CAN DECIDE WHAT COMES NEXT.
TRUTH IS, AT THIS POINT, I JUST WANT TO GO HOME. BACK TO BROOKLYN.
ME TOO.
I BELIEVE WE CAN HELP YOU BOTH. I CAN SEND YOU BACK AND YOU TWO CAN MEND YOUR WAYS.
CAN'T SAY I'LL MISS YOU. WELL, MAYBE A LITTLE.
YOU DID THE RIGHT THING. BOTH OF YOU.
AGREED. WOW, BROOKLYN HASN'T CHANGED A BIT.
WE'RE SORRY, KIDS. WE DIDN'T MEAN TO CAUSE ANY HARM.
AND GOOD LUCK STOPPING GOULD. I GET THE FEELING YOU'LL SEE MORE OF HIM.
ZZZZAP

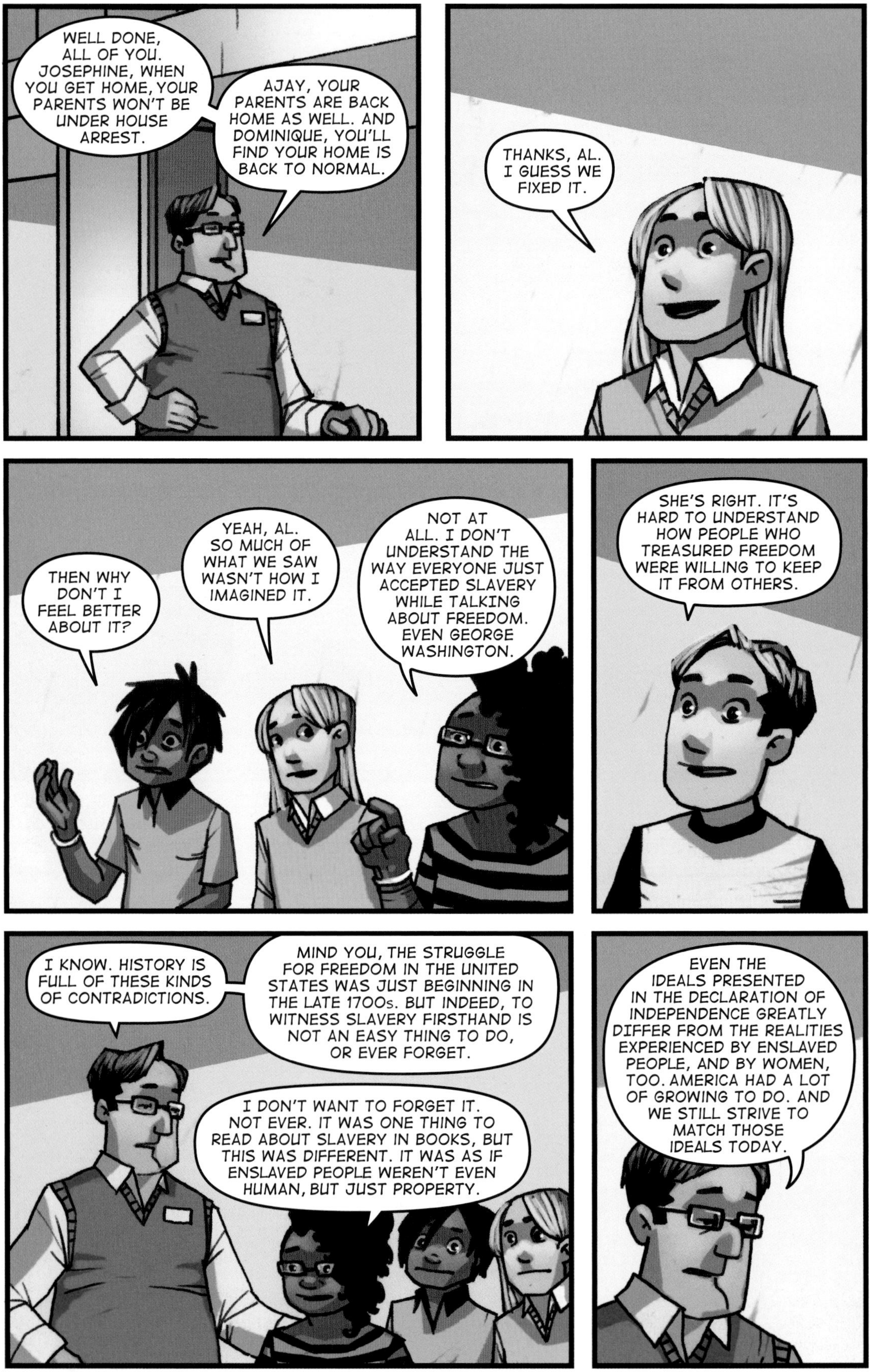
WELL DONE, ALL OF YOU. JOSEPHINE, WHEN YOU GET HOME, YOUR PARENTS WON'T BE UNDER HOUSE ARREST.
AJAY, YOUR PARENTS ARE BACK HOME AS WELL. AND DOMINIQUE, YOU'LL FIND YOUR HOME IS BACK TO NORMAL.
THANKS, AL. I GUESS WE FIXED IT.
THEN WHY DON'T I FEEL BETTER ABOUT IT?
YEAH, AL. SO MUCH OF WHAT WE SAW WASN'T HOW I IMAGINED IT.
NOT AT ALL. I DON'T UNDERSTAND THE WAY EVERYONE JUST ACCEPTED SLAVERY WHILE TALKING ABOUT FREEDOM. EVEN GEORGE WASHINGTON.
SHE'S RIGHT. IT'S HARD TO UNDERSTAND HOW PEOPLE WHO TREASURED FREEDOM WERE WILLING TO KEEP IT FROM OTHERS.
I KNOW. HISTORY IS FULL OF THESE KINDS OF CONTRADICTIONS.
MIND YOU, THE STRUGGLE FOR FREEDOM IN THE UNITED STATES WAS JUST BEGINNING IN THE LATE 1700s. BUT INDEED, TO WITNESS SLAVERY FIRSTHAND IS NOT AN EASY THING TO DO, OR EVER FORGET.
I DON'T WANT TO FORGET IT. NOT EVER. IT WAS ONE THING TO READ ABOUT SLAVERY IN BOOKS, BUT THIS WAS DIFFERENT. IT WAS AS IF ENSLAVED PEOPLE WEREN'T EVEN HUMAN, BUT JUST PROPERTY.
EVEN THE IDEALS PRESENTED IN THE DECLARATION OF INDEPENDENCE GREATLY DIFFER FROM THE REALITIES EXPERIENCED BY ENSLAVED PEOPLE, AND BY WOMEN, TOO. AMERICA HAD A LOT OF GROWING TO DO. AND WE STILL STRIVE TO MATCH THOSE IDEALS TODAY.

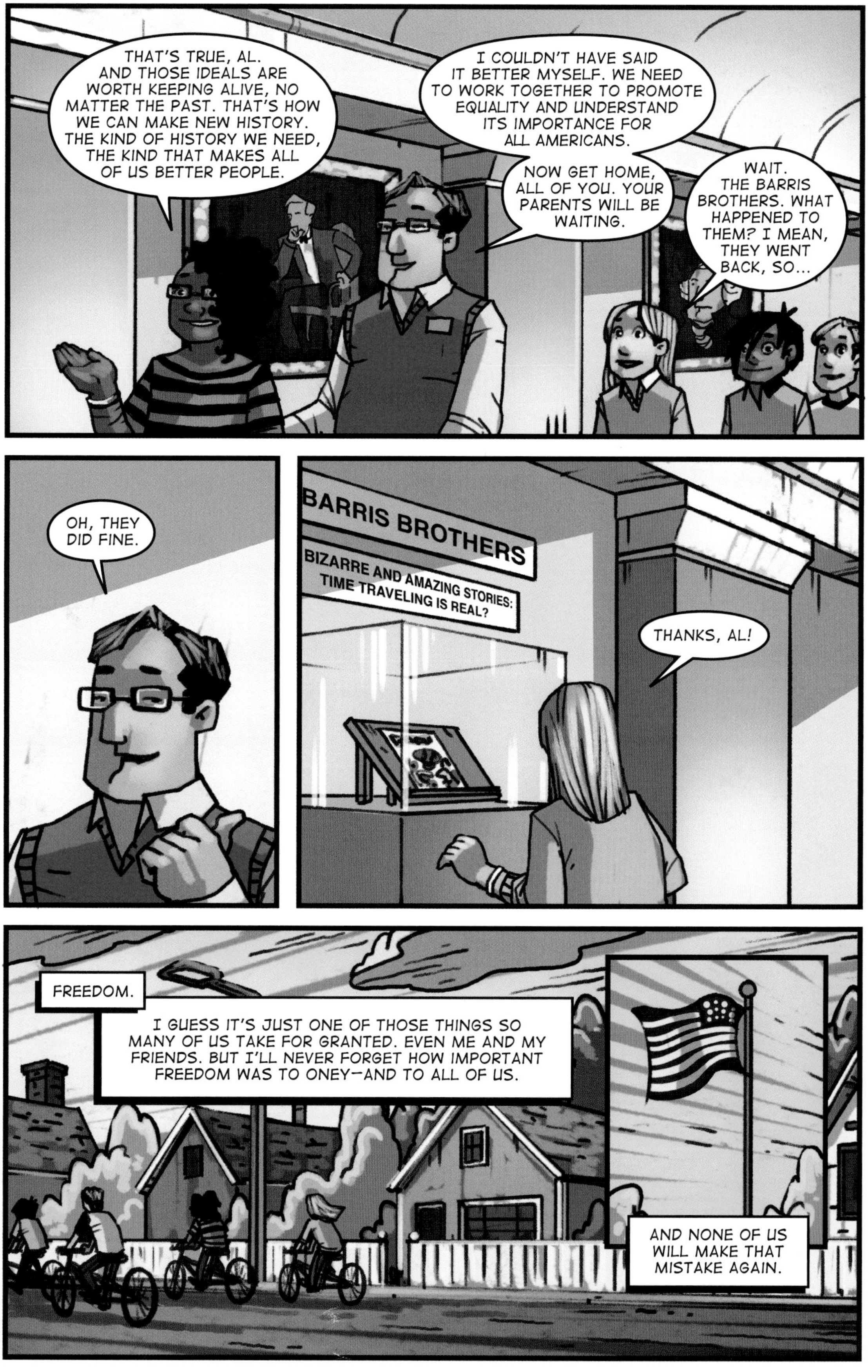
THAT'S TRUE, AL. AND THOSE IDEALS ARE WORTH KEEPING ALIVE, NO MATTER THE PAST. THAT'S HOW WE CAN MAKE NEW HISTORY. THE KIND OF HISTORY WE NEED, THE KIND THAT MAKES ALL OF US BETTER PEOPLE.
I COULDN'T HAVE SAID IT BETTER MYSELF. WE NEED TO WORK TOGETHER TO PROMOTE EQUALITY AND UNDERSTAND ITS IMPORTANCE FOR ALL AMERICANS.
NOW GET HOME, ALL OF YOU. YOUR PARENTS WILL BE WAITING.
WAIT. THE BARRIS BROTHERS. WHAT HAPPENED TO THEM? I MEAN, THEY WENT BACK, SO...
OH, THEY DID FINE.
BARRIS BROTHERS
BIZARRE AND AMAZING STORIES: TIME TRAVELING IS REAL?
THANKS, AL!
FREEDOM.
I GUESS IT'S JUST ONE OF THOSE THINGS SO MANY OF US TAKE FOR GRANTED. EVEN ME AND MY FRIENDS. BUT I'LL NEVER FORGET HOW IMPORTANT FREEDOM WAS TO ONEY—AND TO ALL OF US.
AND NONE OF US WILL MAKE THAT MISTAKE AGAIN.

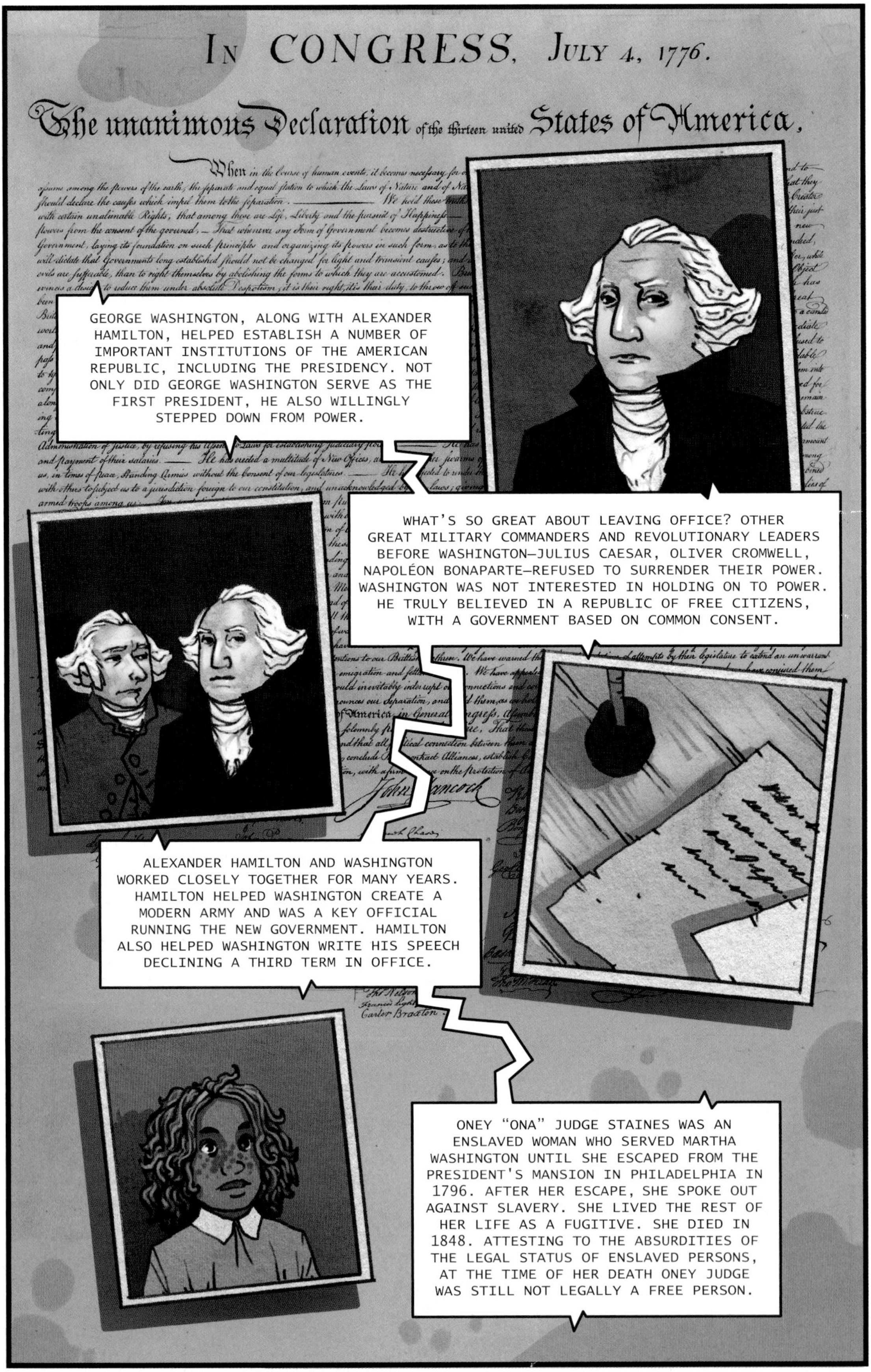
IN CONGRESS, JULY 4, 1776.
The unanimous Declaration of the thirteen united States of America,
GEORGE WASHINGTON, ALONG WITH ALEXANDER HAMILTON, HELPED ESTABLISH A NUMBER OF IMPORTANT INSTITUTIONS OF THE AMERICAN REPUBLIC, INCLUDING THE PRESIDENCY. NOT ONLY DID GEORGE WASHINGTON SERVE AS THE FIRST PRESIDENT, HE ALSO WILLINGLY STEPPED DOWN FROM POWER.
WHAT'S SO GREAT ABOUT LEAVING OFFICE? OTHER GREAT MILITARY COMMANDERS AND REVOLUTIONARY LEADERS BEFORE WASHINGTON—JULIUS CAESAR, OLIVER CROMWELL, NAPOLÉON BONAPARTE—REFUSED TO SURRENDER THEIR POWER. WASHINGTON WAS NOT INTERESTED IN HOLDING ON TO POWER. HE TRULY BELIEVED IN A REPUBLIC OF FREE CITIZENS, WITH A GOVERNMENT BASED ON COMMON CONSENT.
ALEXANDER HAMILTON AND WASHINGTON WORKED CLOSELY TOGETHER FOR MANY YEARS. HAMILTON HELPED WASHINGTON CREATE A MODERN ARMY AND WAS A KEY OFFICIAL RUNNING THE NEW GOVERNMENT. HAMILTON ALSO HELPED WASHINGTON WRITE HIS SPEECH DECLINING A THIRD TERM IN OFFICE.
ONEY "ONA" JUDGE STAINES WAS AN ENSLAVED WOMAN WHO SERVED MARTHA WASHINGTON UNTIL SHE ESCAPED FROM THE PRESIDENT'S MANSION IN PHILADELPHIA IN 1796. AFTER HER ESCAPE, SHE SPOKE OUT AGAINST SLAVERY. SHE LIVED THE REST OF HER LIFE AS A FUGITIVE. SHE DIED IN 1848. ATTESTING TO THE ABSURDITIES OF THE LEGAL STATUS OF ENSLAVED PERSONS, AT THE TIME OF HER DEATH ONEY JUDGE WAS STILL NOT LEGALLY A FREE PERSON.